Tomart's Price Guide to

McDonald's®

Collectibles

By Meredith Williams

Meredith Williams

Edited by Rebecca Sue Trissel

Color Photography by Tom Schwartz

Black & White Photography by Tom Schwartz,
Tom Tumbusch

TOMART PUBLICATIONS
division of Tomart Corporation
Dayton, Ohio

DEDICATION

**To Helen Farrell,
long time McDonald's Corporation employee,
and for the last several years, manager of the McDonald's Archives
... for her dedication to researching Happy Meals in spite of her many other archival duties
... for her patient help with my research and writing of this book.**

ACKNOWLEDGEMENTS

Thanks to God for His love and mercy ... To my mom for developing in me a desire to collect (stamps and coins as a kid) ... To my brothers, Morgan and Martin, who relayed a remark to me which had been told them by Hal Ottaway, that McDonald's items would be good things to collect ... To my wife (Heather) and three sons (Mark, Brian, Nathan) for their patience when I bring stuff home and scatter it all over the house ... To collector friends who have loaned me items to picture in the book: John and Eleanor Larsen, E.J. Ritter, Dick Wilkey, Jim and Rosalie Wolfe, Rich Seidelman, Bill and Pat Poe, Glen McElwee, Ron Wood, Barbara Williams, Myrna Allen, Russ Porter, Kenneth Cassavaugh, Larry Bryant, and the McDonald's Archives ... To Bob Jennings, McDonald's owner in Joplin, his family, managers and employees, for their endurance for the hundreds of times I have come in their stores ... To Lois Dougherty, McDonald's Corporation Archives Technician for her help during my visits there ... To many collector friends all over the U.S. who have shared information with me over the years ... To E.J. Ritter and John and Eleanor Larson for proofreading the text. To E.J. Ritter for all his advice on pricing and for letting me stay at his home during my visits to Chicago.

The color photography is the work of Tom Schwartz, Terry Cavanaugh and Fred Boomer. Page imaging was done by Type One Graphics; color separations by Printing Preparations; printing by Central Printing and Carpenter Lithographing Company. Cover masthead was designed by Fred Blumenthal.

Special thanks to Tom Tumbusch for all the collecting books he has published, for selecting McDonald's Happy Meals as a book to put his time and effort into, and for giving me the chance to write this book. His patience, kindness, endurance and help have been immeasurable ... To T.N. Tumbusch and Bob Welbaum for their production help ... And to Rebecca Trissel for text design and editing.

Published by Tomart Publications, Dayton, Ohio, 45439

Library of Congress Catalog Card Number: 91-67722

ISBN: 0-914293-16-8   Manufactured in the United States of America

1 2 3 4 5 6 7 8 9 0   8 7 6 5 4 3 2 1 9 0

TABLE OF CONTENTS

COLOR PLATES

INTRODUCTION

The McDonald Happy Meal concept wasn't tested until 1977 and didn't go national until 1979, yet thousands of collectors have been actively building large collections. Happy Meal premiums are distributed by the millions. There is usually at least one new one every week and there have been weeks when as many as 12 different regional, test, or clean-up premiums are being distributed somewhere in the U.S.

Often the same premiums are used throughout the world. Then there are foreign premiums never distributed in this country.

If one undertakes to collect Happy Meal memorabilia, there is much more beyond the premiums themselves. Each was normally distributed in a box or sack unless the premium was a container in itself. Then there are all the "point-of-purchase" (POP) promotional materials – signs, displays, translites and similar materials. One could even go as far as taping the TV commercials.

Since 1977 hundreds of millions of Happy Meal items have been produced. A good percentage of the premiums are available at flea markets, swap meets, antique shows, house and garage sales, and similar events. The cost for many is a dollar or less with many more to come as the weeks and months pass. Anyone can easily build an impressive collection featuring their favorite movie, TV, cartoon or toy related heroes.

It's no wonder collecting Happy Meal premiums is one of today's fastest growing hobbies.

Obtaining the colorful boxes, sacks, and promotional materials is a bit more difficult, but material going back several years is readily available. (See page 8).

McDONALD'S: THE BEGINNING

Maurice (Mac) McDonald and his younger brother, Richard (Dick), grew up in New Hampshire. A short time after graduating from high school in the early '30s, Maurice moved to California in search of his future. Later, Richard joined his brother and they were both hired as motion picture studio stagehands. By 1937, they saved enough money to go into business for themselves and opened a small drive-in near a race track in Arcadia, just east of Pasadena.

In 1940, they moved to an octagonal-shaped building at 14th and E Streets in San Bernadino. It was a full menu drive-in with carhops. The business grew and was very successful. But by 1948 the brothers were looking to do away with the carhops and go to a new system based on limited menu, lower prices, volume and speed.

First store in San Bernadino

They closed their drive-in for 3 months in order to make all the necessary changes and reopened at the same location on December 20, 1948. This is the official date of the first limited menu, self-service carry-out McDonald's. Business dropped at first, but after it lost its image as a teenage hangout, families

started coming. The business grew dramatically and attracted attention from people who wanted to copy the McDonald brothers' money-making formula.

By 1952, there were so many people wanting to share in their success, the McDonald brothers decided to franchise their McDonald's Speedee Service System. Their first franchised restaurant was opened May 15, 1953 at 4045 Central in Phoenix, AZ by franchisee Neil Fox. The restaurant had a new look featuring red and white candy-striped tile walls with glowing yellow neon arches going through the roof. By the time Ray Kroc came out to visit the brothers in October 1954, there were 6 additional franchised restaurants operating in California for a total of 8 McDonald's.

A red and white store

The real growth for McDonald's rested in the future of a man from Chicago. Ray Kroc was born on October 5, 1902. His father and mother were Louis and Rose (Hrach) Kroc. Ray was their first child. Four years later his brother, Bob, was born and then sister, Lorraine, three years after Bob.

Ray's father, Louis, was born in Brasy, Bohemia in 1879, the son of an inn proprietor. In 1888, his family came to Chicago. Louis worked for many years for the American District Telegraph Company. The name Kroc is a common name in the Brasy area of Bohemia (40 miles west of Prague). Ray's mother's family also came from Bohemia.

In Ray's younger years he attended the Abraham Lincoln School in Oak Park, a few blocks from home. He attended the Oak Park and River Forest Township High School for two

Ray Kroc

5

years, then joined the American Red Cross Ambulance Drivers Service. The company was moved to Connecticut for departure to France, but never sailed because the armistice for World War I was signed the day they were to leave.

Ray returned to Chicago and played piano for a local radio station at night. During the day, he sold paper cups for the Lilly-Tulip Co. A natural salesman, his next product was the Multimixer which had five stirrers to mix several malts at once. It was the Multimixer which brought Ray Kroc and the McDonald brothers together.

The two brothers ordered several Multimixers and then ordered some more. Ray could not figure out how they were selling so much at a little drive-in, so he went to California to find out.

Ray fell in love with what they were doing, could see lots of potential in their system and became their exclusive national franchising agent. He opened his first store on April 15, 1955 in Des Plaines, IL. In 1961, he bought out the McDonald brothers and began selling franchises. The rest is history.

For more details on the beginning of McDonald's and the rest of the story, read *Grinding It Out, The Making of McDonald's* by Ray Kroc, published by Contemporary Books and *McDonald's, Behind the Arches* by John F. Love, published by Bantam Books, Inc.

HISTORY OF HAPPY MEALS

McDonald's had tried several meal combo promotions for adults, starting with the All-American Meal in 1961. There had

1964 Archy McDonald Trick or Treat bag

1975 Mayor McCheese bag and premium certificate

also been many efforts at children's promotions prior to the Happy Meal. One of the earliest documented is the Archy McDonald Trick or Treat bag in 1964. It's not certain if this bag was a food container or just a give-away.

In 1975, a Mayor McCheese bag and meal combo was designed for children, "The Honorary Meal of McDonaldland". A cheeseburger, fries, box of McDonaldland cookies were included in the bag, along with a McDonaldland Citizenship Wall Certificate which was the premium. The promotion went okay, but was not repeated.

Color cardboard place mat for 1977 L.A. area zoo meal promotion

The Los Angeles area did a McDonaldland Zoo promotion in the summer of 1977 consisting of a colorful place mat and soft plastic animal made by the Marx toy company. A different animal was offered each week for four weeks and a contribution was made to the Los Angeles Zoo for each zoo meal sold.

McDonald's Happy Meals for children began in 1977. Dick Brams, the St. Louis Regional Advertising Director for McDonald's, asked two advertising agencies in his area to come up with ideas to promote a children's meal.

Dick Brams worked in Los Angeles for several years with various companies before becoming the assistant advertising manager for McDonald's in the San Francisco region. In August of 1974, he became McDonald's St. Louis District Advertising Manager. His area included Nebraska, Missouri, central and southern Illinois and Kansas. In 1977, the St. Louis district became a region and he was now Regional Advertising Manager. The new area was expanded to include Memphis.

Brams had been toying with the idea of a children's meal for over four years before he brought his ideas to his advertising agencies to prepare a presentation for the Corporate Marketing Department. The ideas presented were approved for testing in the St. Louis and Kansas City areas.

The St. Louis advertising agency, Stolz, went to work on the idea and came up with a Fun-to-Go Kids Meal. They developed six Fun-to-Go boxes which included a hamburger or cheeseburger, fries, a McDonaldland cookie sample and a premium. The boxes were designed to include activities and graphics which would appeal to children. Fun-to-Go meals began October 17, 1977 in St. Louis. They sold for 70¢ without a drink.

The premiums were generic McDonald's kids items. The test ran for one year until October 16, 1978. Further information is given in the Fun-to-Go section later in the book.

Concurrent with the Fun-to-Go test, the Kansas City advertising agency of Bernstein/Reid and Boasberg was developing and testing their idea for a kids' meal. The agency, which began to represent McDonald's in 1967, had already created pencil puppets, sippy dipper straws, the happy hat, happy cup, happy plate and happy lids, so it was natural for them to develop a Happy Meal.

Bob Bernstein, co-owner, and Dale Pond, his McDonald's account supervisor, hired several famous illustrators to design boxes. Each was given the requirement that there was to be a certain number of activities on each box for kids to do and were to be aimed at children between the ages of four to nine. Each one is quite different because each was designed by a different illustrator.

Dick Brams

The first advertising translite carried this line, "Hamburger, Fries, Soft Drink (each regular size), packet of cookies and Surprise inside the happiest box you ever saw." The price was 99¢ and the test began Nov 4, 1977 in 40-50 stores in the Kansas City area and other McDonald's markets which Bernstein represented.

A surprise or premium was included in each box. The first Happy Meal premium and the first premium specially produced for Happy Meals was a X-O graph card. Four designs were produced with a McDonald's character on the front and a joke on the back. The character on the front moved as you moved the card.

Initially the premiums were ones of low expense. Bob said, "We underestimated the importance of the premium. We thought the box was more important." Later the premium became the main focus in promoting Happy Meals.

The early boxes were beautifully designed and very creative. "The top was rounded with the handle going through the side piece, but this was altered to make them easier for the crew to handle," Bob explained.

Jeff Bremer, on Bernstein's staff, made the first TV commercial for the Happy Meal. "Along with the commercials, we had translites, counter signs, cash register toppers and a T-Shirt which read "Happy Meal makes my tummy giggle" to help advertise," Bob pointed out.

Three tests were run in 1977-78, each using three boxes and McDonaldlized premiums or toys from other companies. The sections, Round Top I, Round Top II, and Round Top III list the boxes and premiums.

When the Fun-to-Go and Happy Meal tests were finished, Dick Brams took the results to McDonald's corporate headquarters in Chicago. After weighing the results, McDonald's decided to try the Happy Meal concept on a national basis.

Dick Brams has been recognized by McDonald's as the "Father of the Happy Meal." Helen Farrell, McDonald's Archivist writes, "He was the creative force behind the development of the concept and was the catalyst for the evolution of the Happy Meal from a local market promotion into McDonald's most successful on-going national children's promotion."

The Bernstein/Rein and Boasberg agency was awarded the McDonald's Corporation Achievement Award for Excellence in Children's Marketing in 1978 for the development of Happy Meals. A beautiful engraved crystal bowl commemorating this honor is on display at the agency. The Happy Meal is the only item on the McDonald's menu board developed by a local advertising agency.

The McDonald's Corporation took the Happy Meal national in June, 1979 with the Happy Meal Circus Wagon promotion. The first big licensed program was "Star Trek – The Motion Picture", used in 1980. Since then, virtually every major licensed character and toy premium appealing to children five

to nine has been used in McDonald's Happy Meals.

THE APPEAL OF HAPPY MEAL COLLECTING

Ever since McDonald's started to include premium toys, books, games, and other items in their children's meals, there has been an interest in collecting them. Collecting McDonald's and other fast-food items was well established by the time the Happy Meal came along in 1977, so a good variety of otherwise "disposable" materials have been preserved.

Collecting the premiums was bound to happen. They are colorful and often associated with top licensed characters ... in addition to the McDonald's characters made famous by TV commercials, playgrounds, and personal appearances.

Beyond the premiums are the boxes, sacks, and other Happy Meal containers. These are much rarer to find, yet just as colorful and collectible.

The point-of-purchase (POP) promotion items varied over the years and are particularly favored by collectors. Initially the product was promoted by hanging displays featuring the boxes. When it was realized the premium was more important than the boxes, signs featuring premiums were attached to the menu board. Then came free-standing counter displays, first as signs, then as 3-dimensional, sometimes motorized displays, containing the premiums. Large cardboard Happy Meal signs were placed in the Message Center, a six-foot fiberboard Ronald McDonald figure made to appear as if he was holding the sign. On the menu board were placed back lighted signs called translites. These first came in two sizes – large for in-store and drive-thru use and later, only in small for the new restyled drive-thru menu board. Depending on the promotion, a variety of smaller materials, such as two-sided tent-like table signs, cash register toppers, tray liners, and similar promotion items, were used. The reader will find these described in detail in the Glossary and listed with the appropriate Happy Meal.

All Happy Meal promotions known to the author at the time of publication are listed in alphabetical order. Each has been given a code number. The Table of Contents and cross references throughout the book aid the reader in finding the material of interest.

Cardboard sign insert for large life-size Ronald McDonald message center sign seen on page 49 in color.

7

VALUABLE COLLECTOR INFORMATION

One of the most commonly overlooked areas of Happy meal collecting is the "Under 3" premium. This is normally a one-piece item with no loose or moving parts, carrying out the theme of the promotion. In rare cases, a "stock" tub toy was used in more than one or a non-related promotion. These are noted throughout the text. The "Under 3" premiums are often missed because they are not normally pictured or displayed. The only reference is a message on promotional materials notifying the patron to ask for special toys or alternate items for children under 3. These special items have been available since 1982 when the premiums had to be recalled due to safety concerns. Special "Under 3" premiums normally come packaged in polybags with zebra stripe markings around the outside border of the package.

Beware of repackaged premiums. Some dealers, realizing a packaged premium is more valuable, are rebaging loose premiums in plain polybags. Most original bags had an insert card or printed polybag. Rarely did a premium come in a plain bag. The correct type of bag is identified for each Happy Meal.

KEEPING UP WITH "WHAT'S NEW!"

This is easy during national promotions ... just visit your local McDonald's and enjoy a Happy Meal. However, not all Happy Meal promotions are national.

There are certain periods during the year when regional or local groups of McDonald's owners meet to vote on the Happy Meal options they feel would be best for their areas. These are called "national option" or "open window" periods. When the supply of material for a given promotion runs short, a back-up supply of "clean-up" materials is always ready for use so the Happy Meal product always remains available. "Clean-up" premiums and packaging is sometimes used instead of the national option or in an open window period.

Regional promotions are sometimes used to tie-in with a major cause or promotional opportunity. Some examples are Black History Week in Detroit or MetroZoo in Miami, FL and promotional tie-ins like the ones done with Sea World and the Dallas Cowboys.

Part of the fun of McDonald's Happy Meal collecting is keeping up with what's new. Friendships have been formed among collectors around the country to acquire extras exclusive to the local McDonald's to trade for items not offered in their area.

The *Collecting Tips Newsletter* is one publication reporting on different Happy Meal offers around the country.

Publications

Toy Shop features a classification for Fast-Food. Here you will find ads for dealers and small private classified ads offering specific Happy Meal items for sale. To obtain subscription information, contact *Toy Shop*, Circulation Department, 700 E. State St., Iola, WI 54990-0001.

Collecting Tips Newsletter on McDonald's collecting features Happy Meal collectibles in each monthly issue. For subscription and advertising information, write *Collecting Tips Newsletter*, P.O. Box 633, Joplin, MO 64802.

Shows

There is an annual convention sponsored by the McDonald's Collector's Club, held each April. The club address changes with the officers so refer to the *Collecting Tips Newsletter* for information.

HOW TO USE THIS BOOK

Tomart's Price Guide to McDonald's Happy Meal Collectibles was designed to be an authoritative and easy to use reference guide. It utilizes an identification and classification system designed to create a standard identification number for each individual figure and associated item.

The format is based on the name of the Happy Meal promotion as identified by the McDonald's package. Code numbers were created based on the first two letters of the series title.

If, for example, you want to locate a Bambi, flip through the book until you find classification numbers beginning with *BA* and read the alphabetical category heading until you reach *Bambi*.

Each item was assigned a reference code number consisting of two letters and four numbers. Use of these numbers in dealer and distributor ads and collector's correspondence is encouraged. Permission for such use to conduct buying, selling and the trade of Happy Meal items in lists, letters or ads is hereby granted. All rights for reporting values in newsletters, advisory services or other collector guides are reserved.

The identity code numbers also serve to match the correct

ACQUIRING McDONALD'S HAPPY MEAL PROMOTIONAL ITEMS

Getting Happy Meal premiums, boxes and sacks is easy, just order a Happy Meal. Getting promotional items is more difficult because there is only one set per McDonald's. As the number of collectors grows, distribution is becoming more of a problem to store owners and managers. In some cases they now have a policy not to give out promotional materials because aggressive collectors have caused unpleasant situations. Understanding will yield more materials than making demands or arguing with the owner or manager in charge.

Most McDonald's stores are operated by independent owners. When a store has sold all its premiums, they usually get rid of the promotional items. Employees often have first choice, so getting a job at McDonald's could be the best way to acquire them. Many store owners or managers are collectors themselves, so these materials don't get very far.

Members of the general public acquire these items according to the policies of individual McDonald's. In rare cases, the first person who asks gets the prize. Names are often written on the backs of displays for the person to pick-up the day after the promotion has concluded. Some stores distribute these materials by drawings or to reward those who make contributions to Ronald McDonald House.

First, you need to determine the policy of your McDonald's and respond accordingly – always remembering to be polite and understanding, even if you are unsuccessful.

listing to a nearby photo. Usually, there is a listing for every photo, but unfortunately, not all items can be depicted. Some items in this volume have been previously listed in other publications by Tomart. This book utilizes a code system which is inconsistent with other Tomart guides.

Premiums are listed in the order in which they were released or in numeric order when this information is known; otherwise they are listed alphabetically.

THE VALUES IN THIS PRICE GUIDE

This book is a collector's guide to average prices, in a range of conditions. The real value of any collectible is what a buyer is willing to pay. No more. No less. Prices are constantly changing – up and down.

Many factors have a bearing on each transaction. Values rise and fall at the whim of collector's willingness to pay the asking price. And there is no guarantee additional items won't be produced in the future. McDonald's has and probably will continue to reuse items in the future.

Trading history for many of the items listed in this book is virtually non-existent. In this case, values have been based on items of similar rarity and desirability. No doubt publication of this photo history will have an impact as collectors see items they would like to own.

However, at this time there is no liquid market for a large collection of Happy Meal collectibles. Except for a limited number of high demand items, the process of turning a good size collection back into cash can be long and expensive.

Collecting should be pursued for the interest and satisfaction involved. There are much better investments at most financial institutions. *Fortune, Business Week* and other business publications have done extensive articles on the pitfalls of speculating in what these magazines categorize as "exotic investments."

Every attempt has been made to have this price guide reflect the market in its broadest sense. The research effort covers extensive travel and consultation with active collectors. The values in this edition are a compilation of information received through March 1992.

CONDITION

The value ranges in this book are based on condition. Let there be no mistake about the price spreads set down on the following pages. The top price refers to a mint, like new, premium in its original packaging, free of any defects whatsoever, selling in a top market.

The low end price describes items in "good" condition. That means, first and foremost, the item is complete with all parts intact. It has been played with, but doesn't show excessive wear. The value of poor condition items would obviously be less than the lowest price shown.

The range between "good" and "as new" is the condition in which most items will be found. "Very good" and "fine" are the most common grades used. In general a "fine" condition item will be one with only minor wear, marks, scratches, blemishes, etc. The item has been in circulation – used, but given care. The value would be somewhat less than the average in the price range as true "as new" items command a premium.

The general guidelines established here, together with the careful noting of any defects when describing a Happy Meal collectible should prove sufficient for most evaluations.

Location also has some influence on price. In Los Angeles and New York, prices are often substantially higher.

Rarity, condition and the amount of material available in the market place all have a direct effect on value. The overriding factor, however, is the number of individuals who wish to acquire any given title and have the money to satisfy their desire.

All prices shown in this book are U.S. dollar values with the dollar signs removed to avoid repetition.

Williard Scott, weatherman on The Today Show appeared as the first Ronald McDonald in this costume.

GLOSSARY

Clean–Up – A time when the stores use left-over boxes/sacks and premiums from past promotions. A time when the toy and box might not match. Several clean-up weeks are scheduled each year.

Copyright Date – The legal protection notification printed on licensed character premiums – seldom having anything to do with the actual dates used.

Counter Card - A sign which sits on the counter and advertises or gives information about a promotion.

Counter Display – In order for young people to see the premiums, counter displays are produced which hold the toys.

Counter Mat – Another promotional item which lies on the counter in view of people ordering.

Generic – A premium or box which can be used for a variety of promotions. Not theme oriented.

Header Card – For several years in the early to middle '80s, stores received a header card with their point-of-purchase (POP) kit. It was used to go on top of the permanent display stand which sat on the counter. For each Happy Meal, the dangling boxes would be changed to keep the display current. The header card and boxes could also be used as ceiling dangler.

Insert Card – The card inside a clear polybag which gives information about the name of the promotion, the name of the premium, the copyright information and safety warning.

Lobby Display – Floor display in the lobby area. Some times these were large cardboard signs or a counter display placed on a stand.

Lug–On – A sign added to a menu board to give extra information. There have been lug-ons which show premiums, hold premiums, say "Available Now", or give pricing or coming soon date information.

McDonaldland – An imaginary place where all the McDonald's characters live.

Menu Board – The large display board above the counter which tells the menu and prices. Spaces are left for advertising translites to be also placed there.

Message Center and Inserts – Early '80s life-size Ronald McDonald fiberboard display to hold cardboard sign inserts advertising the current Happy Meal promotion. This idea was revised in March 1992 to house premium displays.

Mint in Package (MIP) – An item which is in its original package which has never been opened.

Motion – Indicates the counter display operated with a battery and there was some part of the display that moved.

Open Window – A time when McDonald's supply companies create and market Happy Meals. Each region, area, or local owner decides what they want to offer. An open window time is usually scheduled once or twice a year.

Point-of-Purchase – An item which points people to an item in hopes they will purchase it; for example, a translite, counter display, register topper.

Promotions – National/Regional – Many times when you see a Happy Meal promotion you tend to think it is being done everywhere. Many Happy Meals are national, but there are also regional and local Happy Meals (see Open Window)

PVC – soft plastic commonly used for molding figures.

Register Topper – A small advertising piece which affixes to the top of the cash register.

Safety Warning – A message printed on a polybag or insert card to indicate safety tested age group for normal children.

Table Tent – Small triangular shaped signs on tables.

Test – Some Happy Meal items are tested before they are used. The test is to find out how well they sell and if there needs to be an adjustment in design to make the toy more attractive or safer.

Translite – A rear lit transparent sign used on menu boards and drive-thrus.

Unconfirmed – McDonald's toys found which look like they came from a Happy Meal, but proof that they were from a Happy Meal has not been found.

Under 3 – Items which are safety tested as being suitable for children under 3 years of age. The U.S. Government requires that "Under 3" items be available.

X-O Graph – An item which when moved shows a different picture or scene then the original one. Usually there are two views.

Zebra Stripes – Used to identify packaged premiums suitable for children under 3.

IMPORTANT GUIDELINES FROM THE AUTHOR

1. Please read all the comments about each Happy Meal for complete information (the descriptive paragraph and the listings).

2. The lower price means: Complete in good condition and the higher price: 100% Mint or Mint in Package (MIP).

3. Please let me know of any information which would be helpful for future additions.

4. Have fun, but please remember that our relationships to God, to our families, and to one another are far more important than any of these things. After all, they are only toys. Thanks, Meredith Williams, Author, Box 633, Joplin, Missouri 64802.

AD8013   AD8012   AD8011

AD8016   AD8015   AD8014

ADVENTURES OF RONALD McDONALD, 1981

A four-week national promotion from May 25 to June 21, 1981 featured Ronald in a comic strip type adventure scene on the back of the six boxes. The box titles read only "Happy Meal", but the translite included the wording "Collect all six adventures" and "A prize in every box." No specific premium was produced. It was recommended to stores they purchase Ronald/McDonaldland character-oriented premiums from such McDonald's supply companies as M-B Sales and K-Promotions. Some areas used soft or hard rubber McDonaldland figures. These came in 5 colors: blue, green, orange, pink, yellow.

Premiums

AD8001	Big Mac, soft rubber character figure	1 - 4
AD8002	Captain, soft rubber character figure	1 - 4
AD8003	Grimace, soft rubber character figure	1 - 4
AD8004	Hamburglar, soft rubber character figure	1 - 4
AD8005	Mayor McCheese, soft rubber character figure	1 - 4
AD8006	Ronald McDonald, soft rubber character figure	1 - 4
AD8007	Big Mac, hard rubber character figure	2 - 5
AD8008	Captain, hard rubber character figure	2 - 5
AD8009	Grimace, hard rubber character figure	2 - 5
AD8010	Hamburglar, hard rubber character figure	2 - 5
AD8011	Mayor McCheese, hard rubber character figure	2 - 5
AD8012	Ronald McDonald, hard rubber character figure	2 - 5
AD8013	Birdie, hard rubber character figure	2 - 5

Boxes

AD8011	Express	4 - 8
AD8012	Hide n' Seek	4 - 8
AD8013	Kaboom!	4 - 8
AD8014	Rainbow	4 - 8
AD8015	Rodeo	4 - 8
AD8016	Speech	4 - 8

Point of Purchase

AD8025	Translite, menu board	10 - 20

AD8025

AIRPLANE, 1982

This was a 1982 international promotion (Australia, Hong Kong, Latin America, New Zealand, and Sweden), but was used in some limited markets in the U.S. Wings were inserted into slots through the boxes (6 produced) to form an airplane.

AI6011–16

AD8001   AD8002   AD8003   AD8004   AD8005   AD8006

Boxes

AI6011	Big Mac	15 - 30
AI6012	Grimace	15 - 30
AI6013	Hamburglar	15 - 30
AI6014	Mayor McCheese	15 - 30
AI6015	Ronald	15 - 30
AI6016	Ronald/Hamburglar/Mayor McCheese	15 - 30

Point of Purchase

AI6025	Translite	15 - 25

AIRPORT, 1986

Each premium ran for two weeks during this ten-week national Happy Meal promotion from Mar 10 to May 18, 1986. They all carried a 1986 copyright except the helicopter which was marked 1982. The premium pieces came attached

to a plastic tree. Two "Under 3" premiums were suggested, others could have been used. The "Under 3" premiums were produced in other colors than those listed below and were sold by the supply company to McDonald's stores for use at birthday parties or as give-aways. The Big Mac Helicopter was produced as a give-away in 1982 in red and blue, but the green color was produced and used exclusively in the 1986 Happy Meal. There were 4 boxes, each featuring interesting aviation facts.

AI6061   AI6065   AI6062   AI6064   AI6063

11

Premiums

AI6061	Big Mac Helicopter, green, 3 pcs, #1	2 - 5
AI6062	Fry Guy Flyer, blue, 3 pcs, #2	2 - 5
AI6063	Ronald McDonald Seaplane, red, 4 pcs, #3	2 - 5
AI6064	Grimace Ace, purple, 4 pcs, #4	2 - 5
AI6065	Birdie Bent Wing Blazer, pink, 5 pcs, #5	2 - 5
AI6066	Fry Guy Friendly Flyer, blue (Under 3)	1 - 2
AI6067	Grimace Smiling Shuttle, blue (Under 3)	1 - 2

Boxes

AI6075	Control Tower	1 - 3
AI6076	Hangar	1 - 3
AI6077	Terminal	1 - 3
AI6078	Luggage Claim Area	1 - 3

Point of Purchase

AI6085	Translite, menu board/drive-thru (large)	6 - 10
AI6086	Translite, drive-thru (small)	5 - 8
AI6087	Message Center Insert	6 - 10
AI6088	Menu Board Premium Lug-On	4 - 6

ALVIN & THE CHIPMUNKS, 1991

This regional promotion ran in Minnesota and Texas, March 8 – April 12, 1991. The premiums were designed with costumes from past and future eras and each came with an accessory. Brittany was dressed in a Poodle Skirt from the '50s; Alvin in a '60s rock costume; Theodore in a black tie outfit from the '80s; Simon in a space age outfit from the '90s. All premiums came in a clear polybag with a color insert card. Inside each bag was a discount coupon towards the purchase of Alvin–related items at Target stores. One sack design was used.

Premiums

AL4001	Alvin/Electric Guitar	3 - 6
AL4002	Brittany/Juke Box	3 - 6

AI6085

AL4001–05

AL4011

AI6067

AI6066

AI6078   AI6077

AI6075   AI6076   AL4027

AL4025

AL4003	Simon/Video Camera	3 - 6
AL4004	Theodore/Rap Machine	3 - 6
AL4005	Alvin/Juke Box, 1 pc (Under 3)	3 - 6
AL4008	Target Coupon	1 - 3
Sack, white, 7" x 14"		
AL4011	Alvin	1 - 2
Point of Purchase		
AL4025	Translite, menu board	8 - 12
AL4026	Translite, drive-thru	6 - 8
AL4027	Counter Card w/premiums	40 - 60

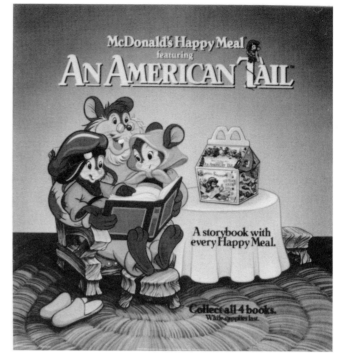

AN5020

AN5004

AN5003

AN5001

AN5002

AN5010   AN5011

AN AMERICAN TAIL, 1986

This Happy Meal was a tie-in with Steven Spielberg's full-length feature animation film, *An American Tail*. The movie was released over Thanksgiving weekend and the Happy Meal ran from Nov 28 thru Dec 24, 1986. The movie was the story of the Mousekowitz family leaving Russia for America in 1886. The premiums consisted of four 24-page storybooks, 7" x 7". The books were exclusive to McDonald's and included all new stories which were expanded versions of events in the movie. Two boxes were used in this offer.

Premiums

AN5001	Fievel's Boat Trip, pink	1 - 3
AN5002	Fievel's Friends, yellow	1 - 3
AN5003	Fievel and Tiger, purple	1 - 3
AN5004	Tony and Fievel, blue-green	1 - 3

Boxes

AN5010	Mouse in the Moon	1 - 3
AN5011	Slippery Solutions	1 - 3
Point of Purchase		
AN5020	Translite, menu board/drive-thru (large)	6 - 10
AN5021	Translite, drive-thru (small)	4 - 8
AN5022	Message Center Insert	6 - 10

ARCHIES (See NEW ARCHIES, 1988)

ASTROSNIKS, 1983

The St. Louis region ran the AstroSniks for eight weeks in 1983. The 8 figures used in this promotion did not come in polybags, but each had a small white paper safety sticker placed on the back of each head. The sticker read "Safety tested for

13

| AS7701 | AS7702 | AS7703 | AS7704 | AS7705 | AS7706 | AS7707 | AS7708 |

children 3 and above, made in Hong Kong." A yellow *M* was on the front of each AstroSnik and molded in the bottom of the feet was "McDonald's, Hong Kong, '83 Bully-Figuren, AstroSnik." Four boxes were utilized.

AS7715–17

AS7718

Premiums

AS7701	Astralia	3 - 8
AS7702	Laser	3 - 8
AS7703	Robo	4 - 9
AS7704	Scout	3 - 8
AS7705	Skater	3 - 8
AS7706	Snikapotamus	4 - 9
AS7707	Sport	3 - 8
AS7708	Thirsty	3 - 8

Boxes

AS7715	AstroSnik Rover, one-wheel	4 - 10
AS7716	Round Space Vehicle	4 - 10
AS7717	Spaceship/Dinosaur	4 - 10
AS7718	Spaceship/Golf Course	4 - 10

Point of Purchase

AS7720	Translite, menu board/drive-thru (large)	10 - 20
AS7721	Tray Liner	2 - 4
AS7722	Table Tent	2 - 4

ASTROSNIKS, 1984

The AstroSniks returned in March/April or August 10 – Sept. 23, 1984. This time there were 6 figures and each came in a zip-lock bag with "safety tested for children 3 years and over" information on it. Included in each bag was a coupon for $4 off on the purchase of an AstroSnik Spacemobile. This coupon needed to be accompanied by 4 McDonald's Cosmic coupons. One was included in each coupon flier. In the IL, MO, NE, and TN regions, "'84 Bully-Figuren™ AstroSnik, McDonald's, Hong Kong" was molded onto the under-base of each one and the yellow *M* was molded onto the front of each figure. However, in the New England area, the message was printed in white on the under-base and the yellow *M* was painted on the front. Two boxes were designed, each one featured 3 cut-out trading cards on the back. Each of the 6 cards featured 1 of the AstroSnik premiums.

Premiums

| AS7731 | Copter, #1, molded | 3 - 8 |

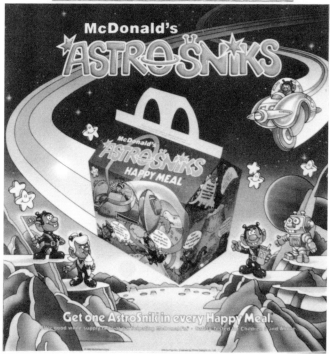

AS7720

AS7732   AS7731   AS7735   AS7736   AS7733   AS7734

AS7721

AS7763

AS7760

Printed (AS7737)

AS7750

AS7751

AS7775

AS7703 w/sticker

AS7732	Racing, #2, molded	3 - 8
AS7733	Ski, #3, molded	3 - 8
AS7734	Commander, #4, molded	3 - 8
AS7735	Drill, #5, molded	3 - 8
AS7736	Perfido, #6, molded	3 - 8
AS7737	Copter, #1, printed	5 - 10
AS7738	Racing, #2, printed	5 - 10
AS7739	Ski, #3, printed	5 - 10
AS7740	Commander, #4, printed	5 - 10
AS7741	Drill, #5, printed	5 - 10
AS7742	Perfido, #6, printed	5 - 10

Boxes

| AS7750 | McDonald's Store | 3 - 8 |
| AS7751 | Snik Earth Station | 3 - 8 |

Point of Purchase

AS7760	Translite, menu board/drive-thru (large)	10 - 15
AS7761	Floor Display, 4-ft AstroSnik character	20 - 25
AS7762	Table Tent	2 - 4
AS7763	Tray Liner	2 - 4

AS7777   AS7779   AS7772   AS7778

These figures were the same as those which are still being sold in retail stores, except the ones for McDonald's came in a zip-lock polybag with the following notice, "This toy in this package has been safety tested for children age 3 years and over. Made in Hong Kong." There was no McDonald's identification on the figures. The 2 boxes used in this promotion were the same as those used in the 1984 campaign (see AS7750 & AS7751).

ASTROSNIKS, 1985

Oklahoma featured 11 AstroSniks in November, 1985.

Premiums

| AS7771 | Banner | 1 - 10 |

AS7772	C.B.	1 - 10
AS7773	Commander	1 - 10
AS7774	Jet	1 - 10
AS7775	Junior	1 - 10
AS7776	Laser	1 - 10
AS7777	Perfido	1 - 10
AS7778	Pyramido	1 - 10
AS7779	Robo	1 - 10
AS7780	Snikapotamus	1 - 10
AS7781	Astralia	1 - 10

Point of Purchase

| AS7795 | Large Counter Card | 10 - 15 |

BI2001   BI2002   BI2003   BI2004   BI2005   BI2006   BI2007

poster with any Bambi collection purchase from Sears. The "Under 3" premiums were not poseable. Each of the 4 boxes could be cut apart and assembled into a Bambi playset. The counter display unit was battery operated.

Premiums

BA2001	Bambi, Set 1	2 - 5
BA2002	Flower, Set 2	2 - 5
BA2003	Friend Owl, Set 3	2 - 5
BA2004	Thumper, Set 4	2 - 5
BA2005	Bambi, with butterfly on tail (Under 3)	3 - 6
BA2006	Bambi, without butterfly (Under 3)	3 - 6
BA2007	Thumper (Under 3)	3 - 6

Boxes

BA2010	Fall	2 - 4
BA2011	Spring	2 - 4
BA2012	Summer	2 - 4
BA2013	Winter	2 - 4

Point of Purchase

BA2020	Translite, menu board	6 - 10
BA2021	Translite, drive-thru	4 - 8
BA2022	Counter Display w/premiums, motion	90 - 140
BA2023	Ceiling Dangler, each character	3 - 5

BAND (See McDONALDLAND BAND, 1986)

BAMBI, 1988

This July 8 to Aug 4, 1988 Happy Meal was a tie-in with the re-release of the 1942 Walt Disney film classic, *Bambi*, based on the story by Felix Salten. Four poseable characters with moveable limbs or wings came in a clear polybag with an insert card. Some cards featured information regarding a free Bambi

AS7795

BA2020

BA2010   BA2011   BA2012

BA2013

BA4032

BARBIE/HOT WHEELS, 1990, Test

The Savannah, GA area was the site for the test market in July, 1990 of a Happy Meal with toys made by Mattel. Four Barbie figures and 4 Hot Wheels were offered. These same items are also available in retail stores. Each premium came in a polybag with an insert card. The Barbie package included a paper diorama backdrop scene to match events where Barbie was appearing. Two different boxes were used, each box had Barbie and Hot Wheels on 2 sides.

Premiums - Barbie
BA4001	Movie Star, pink dress/stars, #1	1 - 20
BA4002	In Concert, black dress, #2	1 - 20
BA4003	Tea Party, dark pink dress, #3	1 - 20
BA4004	Moonlight Ball, light pink gown, #4	1 - 20

Premiums - Hot Wheels
BA4011	Corvette Convertible, white, #1	1 - 20
BA4012	Ferrari, red, #2	1 - 20
BA4013	Hot Bird, silver, #3	1 - 20
BA4014	Camaro Z-28, turquoise, #4	1 - 20

Boxes
BA4020	In Concert/Garage	4 - 8
BA4021	Movie Star/Road Race	4 - 8

Point of Purchase
BA4030	Translite, menu board	10 - 20
BA4031	Translite, drive-thru	8 - 15
BA4032	Counter Display w/premiums	200 - 400

BA4004

BA4002

BA4003

BA4001

BA4014   BA4013   BA4012   BA4011

BA4030

17

BARBIE/HOT WHEELS, 1991

The national Barbie/Hot Wheels promotion, Aug 2–29, 1991, featured different premiums than those used in the test market a year before. This Happy Meal featured several firsts: 1) the first national Happy Meal to have 16 different premiums, 2) the first national Happy Meal to have separate premiums for girls and boys and 3) the first national promotion for Barbie figures (McDonald's or any other company).

The 8 miniatures of the Barbie dolls were exclusive to McDonald's. Each one included a $1 off coupon toward a Barbie doll purchase. "Made for McDonald's, ©1991 Mattel Inc, made in China" plus an identification number appeared on each doll. Dolls #2 and #6 were also used as the "Under 3" premiums and had pink/white zebra stripes around their package.

The 8 Hot Wheels came packaged with a $2 off coupon toward the purchase of a Hot Wheel. The series was California Custom Hot Wheels available in retail stores and were not exclusive to McDonald's. The "Under 3" premium was a tool set. Two boxes were used for Barbie and 2 for the Hot Wheels.

BA4058　BA4057　BA4056　BA4055

BA4062　BA4061　BA4060　BA4059

BA4073　BA4072

BA4070　BA4071

Premiums – Barbie

BA4040	All American, #1		2 - 4
BA4041	Costume Ball, #2		2 - 4
BA4042	Lights and Lace, #3		2 - 4
BA4043	Happy Birthday (Black Barbie), #4		2 - 4
BA4044	Hawaiian Fun, #5		2 - 4
BA4045	Wedding Day Midge, #6		2 - 4
BA4046	Ice Capades, #7		2 - 4
BA4047	My First Barbie (Hispanic Barbie), #8		2 - 4
BA4048	Costume Ball (Under 3)		– – 6
BA4049	Wedding Day (Under 3)		– – 6

Premiums – Hot Wheels

BA4055	'55 Chevy, yellow, #1		2 - 4
BA4056	'63 Corvette, green, #2		2 - 4
BA4057	'57 T-Bird, turquoise, #3		2 - 4
BA4058	Camaro Z-28, purple, #4		2 - 4
BA4059	'55 Chevy, white, #5		2 - 4
BA4060	'63 Corvette, black, #6		2 - 4
BA4061	'57 T-Bird, red, #7		2 - 4
BA4062	Camaro Z-28, orange, #8		2 - 4
BA4063	Tool set: wrench (yellow) & hammer (red) (Under 3)		2 - 6

Boxes

BA4070	At Home	1 - 3
BA4071	On Stage	1 - 3
BA4072	Cruising	1 - 3
BA4073	Racers	1 - 3

Point of Purchase

BA4080	Translite, menu board	6 - 10
BA4081	Translite, drive-thru	4 - 8
BA4082	Counter Display w/premiums	75 - 125
BA4083	Tray Liner	1 - 2
BA4084	Crew Button	1 - 2

BA4040　BA4041　BA4042　BA4043

BA4044　BA4045　BA4046　BA4047

BA4063

BA4048

BA4049

BA4080

BA4082   BA5520

BARNYARD, 1986   BA4083

The Barnyard Happy Meal, also known as Old McDonald's Farm, ran in St. Louis and Nashville in Apr – May 1986. Seven poseable farm friends made by the Playmates Co. came polybagged with the following printed on the outside of the bag: "Safety tested for children age 3 and over. Caution: May contain small parts and is not intended for children under 3. Please discard bag." There was no McDonald's identification on the bag or on the premium. The cow, pig and sheep were imprinted "Made in Hong Kong"; the other premiums had no markings. The 2 boxes were of a special design with an extra front flap which folded down to a barn or house scene.

BA4083

BA5515–16

Premiums

BA5501	Cow, white/brown	3 - 8
BA5502	Farmer, white shirt, green pants, brown hat	3 - 8
BA5503	Hen, white	3 - 8
BA5504	Pig, beige	3 - 8
BA5505	Rooster, white	3 - 8
BA5506	Sheep, white	3 - 8
BA5507	Wife, blue dress, yellow hair	3 - 8

Boxes

BA5515	Barn	10 - 20
BA5516	House	10 - 20

Point of Purchase

BA5520	Translite, menu board	10 - 15

BEACH BALL – OLYMPIC, 1984 (unconfirmed)

The 3 beach balls offered were each polybagged (not heat sealed, but with a piece of Scotch tape securing the fold) and bore a 1984 copyright date and the Olympic logo. These have been found in Florida.

BA5501 B5503 BA5504   BA5506 BA5505 BA5502 BA5507

19

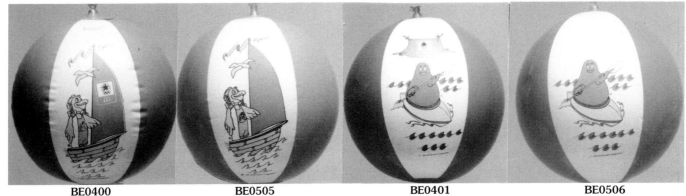

BE0400   BE0505   BE0401   BE0506

BE0552

BE0607

BE0603

BE0507

BE0601

BE0602

BE1150

Premiums
BE0400   Birdie/Sailboat, blue   5 - 10
BE0401   Grimace/Kayak, purple   5 - 10
BE0402   Ronald, red   5 - 10

BEACH BALL, 1985 (unconfirmed)

These beach balls appear to be the same as the 1984 Olympic ones, but they have a 1985 copyright date and no Olympic logo. These too were polybagged with Scotch tape used to secure the end flap.

Premiums
BE0505   Birdie/Sailboat, blue   5 - 10
BE0506   Grimace/Kayak, green   5 - 10
BE0507   Ronald, red   5 - 10

BEACH BALL, 1985, Florida (unconfirmed)

On these beach balls, a Florida logo was added to the 1985 set. The logo was round, yellow and included the name "Florida", 3 palm trees and the McDonald's logo. The premiums were polybagged and the end flap sealed via Scotch tape.

BE0615

| BE1155 | | BE1158 | | BE1156 | | BE1157 | |

Premiums

BE0550	Birdie/Sailboat, blue	3 - 10
BE0551	Grimace/Kayak, green	3 - 10
BE0552	Ronald beach ball, red	3 - 10

BEACH BALL, 1986

A new regional Beach Ball Happy Meal came out in 1986. A single box was used to hold the Happy Meal and the poly-bagged premium (end flap sealed via Scotch tape). This Happy Meal is known to have been used in WA, NY, and CO.

Premiums

BE0601	Birdie/Sand Castle, blue	5 - 10
BE0602	Grimace/Umbrella, yellow	5 - 10
BE0603	Ronald/Waving/Seal, red	5 - 10
Boxes		
BE0607	Beach Scene (postcard)	2 - 5
Point of Purchase		
BE0615	Translite, menu board	8 - 12

BEACH TOY, 1989, Test

This test was run in Greenville, SC in June of 1989. Four inflatable beach toys were offered. Each card inside the polybag read "Collect all 4." Four sacks were used.

Premiums

BE1150	Birdie Seaside Submarine, pink	- - 10
BE1151	Fry Kid Super Sailer, red/purple	- - 10
BE1152	Grimace Bouncin' Beach Ball, yellow	- - 10
BE1153	Ronald Fun Flyer, turquoise	- - 10
Sacks, 8¹/₂" x 12"		
BE1155	Friendly Reflections	2 - 6

| BE1174 | BE1194 | BE1175 |

BE1156	Silly Story	2 - 6
BE1157	Splash Party	2 - 6
BE1158	Submarine Surprise	2 - 6
Point of Purchase		
BE1160	Translite, menu board	10 - 15

BEACH TOY, 1990

The national Beach Toy Happy Meal ran June 1–28, 1990. Four of the 8 premiums had never been offered before: a shovel with sand spinner, a rake which squirted water, an inflatable flying disk and an inflatable submarine. Other new features were see-through panels and sails on the inflatables and transparent sand toys. Each week 1 inflatable toy and 1 plastic toy were offered. The card inside the polybagged inflatables read "Collect all 8." Four sacks were used for 6 of the premiums, the 2 pails served as their own container. Two ceiling danglers, each one featuring 4 of the 8 premiums (2 per side) were involved with this Happy Meal offering. One dangler (BE1193) showed the BE1177, BE1176, BE1171 and BE1170; the other (BE1194) – BE1172, BE1173, BE1174, and BE1175.

Premiums

BE1170	Fry Kid Super Sailer (same as BE1151), Week 1	1 - 4
BE1171	Beach Pail–Ronald/Grimace, transparent w/yellow lid & handle, Week 1	1 - 3
BE1172	Grimace Bouncin' Beach Ball (same as BE1152), Week 2	1 - 4
BE1173	Birdie Shovel/Sand Spinner, red, Week 2	1 - 3
BE1174	Ronald Fun Flyer, (same as BE1153), Week 3	1 - 4
BE1175	Fry Kids Sand Castle Pail, transparent w/red lid & handle, Week 3	1 - 3

| BE1173 | BE1194 | BE1172 |

BE1187   BE1188   BE1186   BE1185

BE1170   BE1193   BE1171

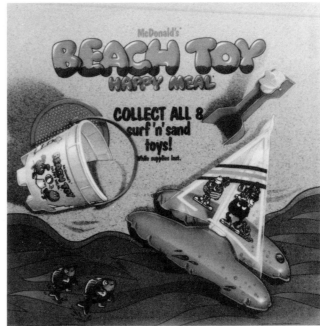

BE1191

BE1177   BE1193   BE1176   BE1550   BE1551   BE1552

BE1176	Birdie Seaside Submarine (same as BE1150), Week 4	1 - 4
BE1177	Ronald Squirt Rake, blue/green, Week 4	1 - 3

Sacks, 8¹/₂" x 12"

BE1185	Grimace	1 - 3
BE1186	Hamburglar	1 - 3
BE1187	Ronald/Stars	1 - 3
BE1188	Ronald/Treasure Chest	1 - 3

Point of Purchase

BE1191	Translite, menu board	8 - 10
BE1192	Translite, drive-thru	6 - 8
BE1193	Ceiling Dangler, 4 premiums	10 - 15
BE1194	Ceiling Dangler, 4 premiums	10 - 15

BEACHCOMBER HAPPY PAIL, 1986

The plastic pails were white with a white lid and handle. Each was copyrighted 1986 and each lid contained four ¹/₂" holes

near the outside edge. A yellow shovel completed the premium. SC is the known area for this offering.

Premiums

BE1550	Grimace	10 - 18
BE1551	Mayor McCheese	10 - 18
BE1552	Ronald	10 - 18

Point of Purchase

BE1556	Translite, menu board	10 - 15

BEDTIME, 1989

This was an national option Happy Meal promotion from

22

BE4011   BE4012

BE4001   BE4002

BE4003   BE4004

BE4010   BE4013

BE4020

Feb 3 – Mar 2, 1989. The first week of the promotion highlighted National Dental Health Month. Procter & Gamble Co.
provided a tube of Sparkle Crest, a super cool gel toothpaste
for kids, to go with the Ronald toothbrush. Four bedtime-relat-
ed items featuring Ronald and 4 boxes comprised this offer.
The wash mitt and night stand figure came in polybags with an
insert card; the toothbrush was polybagged without any card
and the cup was not issued in a polybag. The toothpaste came
in a cardboard box without the pricing bar code. An "Under 3"
premium was only needed during Week 1 and special ship-
ments of the drinking cup were provided stores.

Premiums

BE4001	Toothbrush, yellow, & .85 oz tube of Sparkle Crest, Set 1	2 - 4
BE4002	Drinking Cup, 12 oz, blue, Set 2	1 - 3
BE4003	Foam Wash Mitt, blue, Set 3	2 - 4
BE4004	Night Stand Figure – Ronald/star, glows in the dark, Set 4	2 - 4

Boxes

BE4010	Hidden Slippers	1 - 3
BE4011	Pillow Fight	1 - 3
BE4012	Scavenger Hunt	1 - 3
BE4013	Slumber Party	1 - 3

Point of Purchase

BE4020	Translite, menu board	6 - 10
BE4021	Translite, drive-thru	4 - 8

BERENSTAIN BEARS, 1986, Test

Evansville, IN served as the test market for this promotion
from Nov 28 to Dec 24, 1986. The Bears had been around 25
years, but only since 1985 had they been featured in their own
Saturday morning TV show on CBS. Before that the Bears
were stars of 5 special TV shows and nearly 50 books.
Husband and wife, Stan and Jan Berenstain, created the Bears.

Each of the Bears had a soft rubber texture with flocked
heads and painted hands and feet. No "Under 3" premiums
have been identified. The Papa Bear came with a burnt orange
wheelbarrow. Mama Bear was dressed in a pants suit and came
with a shopping cart. Sister Bear came with a sled and had her
arms down at her sides. Brother Bear came on a yellow scooter
with a green handle. No McDonald's identification was found
on any of the accessories. Each premium came in a polybag
with a 1-color insert card. The 4 boxes bore Christmas motifs.

BE7304   BE7301   BE7302   BE7303

| BE7310 | BE7313 | BE7312 |

| BE7311 | BE7533 | BE7531 |

Premiums		
BE7301	Papa Bear	10 - 15
BE7302	Mama Bear	10 - 15
BE7303	Sister Bear	10 - 15
BE7304	Brother Bear	10 - 15
Boxes (Christmas motif)		
BE7310	Barn	5 - 13
BE7311	General Store	5 - 13
BE7312	Home	5 - 13
BE7313	School	5 - 13
Point of Purchase		
BE7320	Translite, menu board	15 - 20
BE7321	Translite, drive-thru	10 - 12

BERENSTAIN BEARS, 1987

The first national Berenstain Bear Happy Meal ran Oct 31 to Nov 29, 1987. Several modifications were made over the test run. The figures were now of a hard rubber composition. Each had a flocked head, but the hands and feet were of the natural material used, not painted. The 2 "Under 3" premiums were 1-piece figures with no flocking on the head and paper punch-outs. The accessories were now identified as McDonald's. Papa's wheelbarrow and Brother's scooter were now of a different color. Mama wore a dress; while Sister Bear came with a wagon and her arms positioned straight out. All were poly-bagged with a color insert card. The 4 boxes were designed with a fall motif.

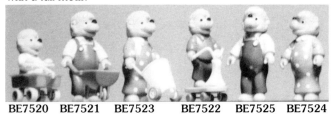

| BE7520 | BE7521 | BE7523 | BE7522 | BE7525 | BE7524 |

BE7542

BE7530   BE7532

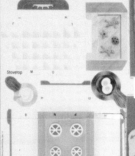

BE7525 – *punch-outs*   BE7524 – *punch-outs*

BE7640   BE7641

BE7643

BE7540

Premiums

BE7520	Sister/Wagon, red, #1	2 - 4
BE7521	Papa/Wheelbarrow, brown, #2	2 - 4
BE7522	Brother/Scooter, green floor, yellow handle, red wheels, #3	2 - 4
BE7523	Mama/Shopping Cart, yellow, #4	2 - 4
BE7524	Mama/Kitchen Paper Punch-outs (Under 3)	3 - 8
BE7525	Papa/Tool Paper Punch-outs (Under 3)	3 - 8

Boxes (Fall motif)

BE7530	Barn Dance	1 - 3
BE7531	General Store	1 - 3
BE7532	School	1 - 3
BE7533	Tree House	1 - 3

Point of Purchase

BE7540	Translite, menu board/drive-thru (large)	6 - 10
BE7541	Translite, drive-thru (small)	4 - 8
BE7542	Counter Display w/premiums	50 - 80
BE7543	Crew Button, metal	1 - 2

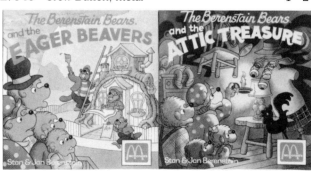

BE7631   BE7627

BE7650

BE7644   BE7645

BE7629   BE7625

BE7642

BERENSTAIN BEARS BOOKS, 1990

The second national Berenstain Bear Happy Meal promotion featured activity and storybooks and ran Jan 26 – Feb 22, 1990. The 4 storybooks were full-color, 24 pages and 7" x 7". The 4 activity books measured 8" x 10". All were written exclusively for McDonald's and included the McDonald's logo on the front. Four boxes were used nationally and two colored bags which measured 7" x 13½" were tested in South Bend, IN.

BE7628   BE7632

Premiums

BE7625	Life with Papa, storybook, Week 1	1 - 3
BE7626	Life with Papa, activity book, Week 1	1 - 3
BE7627	Attic Treasure, storybook, Week 2	1 - 3
BE7628	Attic Treasure, activity book, Week 2	1 - 3
BE7629	Substitute Teacher, storybook, Week 3	1 - 3
BE7630	Substitute Teacher, activity book, Week 3	1 - 3
BE7631	The Eager Beavers, storybook, Week 4	1 - 3
BE7632	The Eager Beavers, activity book, Week 4	1 - 3

Boxes & Sacks

BE7640	Sharing, box	1 - 3
BE7641	Teamwork, box	1 - 3
BE7642	Thank Goodness, box	1 - 3
BE7643	What to Do, box	1 - 3
BE7644	Teamwork, sack	6 - 10
BE7645	What to Do, sack	6 - 10

Point of Purchase

BE7650	Translite, menu board	6 - 10
BE7651	Translite, drive-thru	4 - 8

BE7630   BE7626

BIGFOOT, 1987

Four Super Monster trucks with 1½" wheels and 4 Monster trucks with 1" wheels were used in the 1987 Bigfoot (Ford) Happy Meal promotion. One truck of each design was issued with a "Ms. Bigfoot" logo on the side to appeal to girls. Each premium came in a clear polybag with a safety sticker inside.

Two different sets have been discovered. The St. Louis region vehicles had no McDonald's identification, but another set found in the Buffalo and Florida areas carried McDonald's identification. One box was used.

BI3030

Premiums
BI3001	Bronco, green, 1½" wheels, w/o M		3 - 6
BI3002	Pick Up, purple, 1½" wheels, w/o M		3 - 6
BI3003	Ms. Pick Up, turquoise, 1½" wheels, w/o M		3 - 6
BI3004	Shuttle, red, 1½" wheels, w/o M		3 - 6
BI3005	Bronco, orange, 1" wheels, w/o M		3 - 6
BI3006	Pick Up, light blue, 1" wheels, w/o M		3 - 6
BI3007	Ms. Pick Up, pink, 1" wheels, w/o M		3 - 6
BI3008	Shuttle, black, 1" wheels, w/o M		3 - 6
BI3009	Bronco, green, 1½" wheels, w/M		4 - 8
BI3010	Pick Up, purple, 1½" wheels, w/M		4 - 8
BI3011	Ms. Pick Up, turquoise, 1½" wheels, w/M		4 - 8
BI3012	Shuttle, red, 1½" whels, w/M		4 - 8
BI3013	Bronco, orange, 1" wheels, w/M		4 - 8
BI3014	Pick Up, light blue, 1" wheels, w/M		4 - 8
BI3015	Ms. Pick Up, pink, 1" wheels, w/M		4 - 8
BI3016	Shuttle, black, 1" wheels, w/M		4 - 8

BI3006	BI3008	BI3005	BI3007
BI3002	BI3003	BI3001	BI3004
BI3014	BI3015	BI3013	BI3016
BI3010	BI3011	BI3009	BI3012

Box
BI3025	Big Foot	2 - 5

Point of Purchase
BI3030	Translite, menu board	8 - 12
BI3031	Translite, drive-thru	6 - 10

BIG TOP, 1988

In 1988, a generic box was produced to be used with birthday parties at McDonald's. Other circus-themed items (hats, napkins, etc) were available. If any premium was given, it would have been a generic.

Box
BI3401	Big Top	1 - 3

BLACK HISTORY, 1988

Parts of Detroit, MI used the Black History Happy Meal in January 1988. The two 8½" x 11" coloring books did not have any McDonald's identification on them. One box used.

Premiums
BL1300	Little Martin, Jr., Vol. 1	15 - 40
BL1301	Little Martin, Jr., Vol. 2	15 - 40

Box
BL1305	Black History	15 - 40

BL1301   BL1300

BI3025   BI3401   BL1305

BOATS 'N FLOATS, 1987

A national promotion using 4 McDonaldized vacuform boats ran from Aug 7 – Sept 3, 1987. Each boat included a top, base and a sticker sheet. The boat served as its own container. Prices shown are for boats with stickers applied.

Premiums

BO1500	Grimace Ski Boat, purple, Week 1	4 - 7
BO1501	Fry Girl, Fry Guys Raft, green, Week 2	4 - 7
BO1502	Chicken McNuggets Lifeboat, orange, Week 3	4 - 7
BO1503	Birdie Float, yellow, Week 4	4 - 7
BO1504	BO1500-03, boat w/o stickers	2 - 5
BO1505	BO1500-03, boat & separate sticker sheet	5 - 10
BO1506	BO1500-03, sticker sheet only	3 - 5

BO1500   BO1502

BO1501   BO1503

BO1510

CA3100   CA3104   CA3101   CA3102

Point of Purchase

BO1510	Translite, menu board	6 - 10
BO1511	Translite, drive-thru	4 - 8

BOO BAGS (see McBOO BAGS, 1991)

CAMP McDONALDLAND, 1990

McDonald's went camping with their summer promotion, May 30 – July 5, 1990. Offered were 4 plastic camping out premiums with the "Under 3" premium being 1 of those offered in the regular Happy Meal. Four box designs were utilized; 2 colored bags (7" x 13^1/$_2$") were test marketed in South Bend, IN.

Premiums

CA3100	Grimace Canteen, blue, 2 pcs, Set 1	1 - 3
CA3101	Birdie Camper/Mess Kit, green, orange handle, 3pcs, Set 2	1 - 3
CA3102	Fry Kid Utensils – knife, purple; fork, turquoise; spoon, yellow. Came w/5 Curad Happy Strips & a 25¢ coupon for Happy Strips, Set 3	1 - 4
CA3103	CA3102 packaged w/o the strips or coupon	- - 8
CA3104	Ronald Collapsible Cup, red, Set 4 (polybagged)	1 - 4
CA3105	Same as CA3104, except packaged in the Black/white zebra striped polybag w/"Under 3" identification	- - 5

Boxes & Sacks

CA3110	At the Lake, box	1 - 3
CA3111	Camping Out, box	1 - 3
CA3112	Nature Walk, box	1 - 3
CA3113	Playtime at Camp, box	1 - 3
CA3114	Playtime, sack	6 - 10
CA3115	Nature Walk, sack	6 - 10

Point of Purchase

CA3120	Translite, menu board	6 - 10
CA3121	Translite, drive-thru	4 - 8

CA3110-11

CA3114   CA3115

CA3112　　　　　　CA3113

CA6310

CA3120

CARNIVAL, 1990

Carnival rides were featured in this regional Happy Meal which ran Sept 7 – Oct 4, 1990 and Mar/Apr 1991. The 4 regular meal premiums were made up of interchangeable parts and came polybagged. One box design was used.

Premiums

CA6300	Birdie/Swing, blue stand, orange arches, red swing, 5 pcs	3 - 7
CA6301	Grimace/Turn-Around, green stand, blue holder, 5 pcs	3 - 7
CA6302	Hamburglar/Ferris Wheel, yellow stand, purple holder, blue handle, orange seat, 5 pcs	3 - 7
CA6303	Ronald/Carousel, red stand, green seats, 4 pcs	3 - 7
CA6304	Grimace on Rocker, purple, 1 pc (Under 3)	4 - 8

Box

CA6310	Ronald/Train	1 - 3

Point of Purchase

CA6315	Translite, menu board	8 - 12
CA6316	Translite, drive-thru	6 - 10
CA6317	Window Decal	2 - 3

CA6315

CASTLEMAKER, 1987

Houston, TX and parts of MI were involved in a regional Happy Meal during the summer of 1987. Each of the 4 sand molds featured a two-piece design – a top and a bottom. An *M* was molded into each premium.

Premiums

CA7500	Cylindrical mold, yellow, 8" round/5" high	10 - 15
CA7501	Domed mold, blue, 8"x8" base/4" high	10 - 15
CA7502	Rectangle mold, red, 8"x4½"/4" high	10 - 15
CA7503	Square mold, dark blue, 5½" base/4" high	10 - 15

Point of Purchase

CA7515	Translite, menu board	10 - 15
CA7516	Translite, drive-thru	8 - 12

CA6300　　　CA6303　　　CA6304　　　CA6301

CA6302

CA7503

CA7501

29

CA1010 - *front*   CA1010 - *back*   CA1011 - *back*

CA7500   CA7502

CH1001   CH1002   CH1003   CH1004   CH1006   CH1005

CHANGEABLES, 1987

Two variations of the promotion featuring food items which changed into robots ran in several regions during 1987. The first Changeable Happy Meal presented 5 premiums, while the later Changeable Happy Meal added a milk shake for premium #6. All figures came in a polybag with a color insert card. Due to the premium number difference, one box showed 5 premiums and another box showed all 6 offerings. (See also NEW FOOD CHANGEABLES, 1989)

Premiums
CH1001	Big Mac Sandwich	2 - 5
CH1002	Chicken McNuggets	2 - 5
CH1003	Egg McMuffin Sandwich	2 - 5
CH1004	Large French Fries	2 - 5
CH1005	Quarter Pounder Sandwich w/cheese	2 - 5
CH1006	Milk Shake	2 - 6

CH1022

Boxes
CH1010	Five Premiums	2 - 4
CH1011	Six Premiums	2 - 3
Point of Purchase		
CH1020	Translite, menu board, 5 premiums	10 - 12
CH1021	Translite, drive-thru, 5 premiums	8 - 10
CH1022	Translite, menu board, 6 premiums	8 - 10
CH1023	Translite, drive-thru, 6 premiums	6 - 8

CHIP 'N DALE RESCUE RANGERS, 1989

This Oct 27 – Nov 23, 1989 Happy Meal was a tie-in with the start of a new Disney TV show, "The Rescue Rangers." The show featured Chip 'N Dale characters plus 2 mouse companions: Gadget and Monterey Jack. Gadget made

CH1020

CH4060   CH4061   CH4062

CH4063

Premiums

CH4050	Chip's Whirly-Cupter, tea cup/button wheels/ruler for blade, Set 1	1 - 4
CH4051	Dale's Roto–Roadster, measuring cup/thimble front piece/pipe & brush propeller, Set 2	1 - 4
CH4052	Gadget's Rescue Racer, tennis shoe/ spatula propeller, Set 3	1 - 4
CH4053	Monterey Jack's Propel-A-Phone, telephone receiver/checkers for front wheels/screws for back wheels/spatula for propeller, Set 4	1 - 4
CH4054	Chip's Rockin' Racer (bottle/brush) (Under 3)	2 - 5
CH4055	Gadget's Rockin' Rider (tea cup) (Under 3)	2 - 5

Boxes

CH4060	Framed	1 - 3
CH4061	Rollin' in Dough	1 - 3
CH4062	Yolk's on Him	1 - 3
CH4063	Whale of a Time	1 - 3

Point of Purchase

CH4070	Translite, menu board	6 - 10
CH4071	Translite, drive-thru	4 - 8
CH4072	Counter Display w/premiums	65 - 95

"Gadgetmobiles" out of common household items to help the characters in their adventures. The 4 Gadgetmobile premiums were of interchangeable parts (the "Under 3" premiums were of 1 piece construction). Four box designs were available.

CH4050   CH4051   CH4052   CH4053   CH4055   CH4054

CH4070

CIRCUS, 1983   CH4072

A circus theme was featured in the Sept 30 – Nov 23, 1983 Happy Meal boxes and premiums and in the Sept/Oct *McDonaldland Fun Times* kid's magazine. The 4 plastic pre-miums were issued in polybags and each came in several colors (1 had 2 different character faces) and the 4 cardboard cut-out sheets (10$\frac{1}{2}$" x 21") interconnected to form a large circus scene complete with midway, tent and animals. Six boxes were designed for this offer.

CI1606

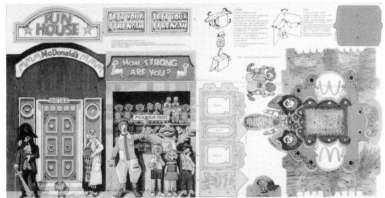

CI1607

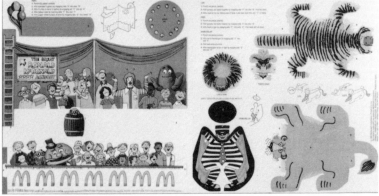

CI1608

CI1609

CI6015

CI6016

CI6017

CI6018

Premiums

CI6001	French Fry Faller, yellow, orange, blue, 4 pcs on tree	6 - 12
CI6002	Fun House Mirror/Ronald, blue, red, yellow, 3 pcs on tree	6 - 12
CI6003	Fun House Mirror/Hamburglar, blue, red, yellow, 3 pcs on tree	6 - 12
CI6004	Grimace Strong Gong, purple, yellow, green,	6 - 12

CI6001   CI6004

CI6019   CI6020

CI6002   CI6003   CI6005

CI6710

CI6701   CI6702   CI6704   CI6703

7 pcs on tree

CI6005	Ronald Acrobat, red, yellow, orange, 6 pcs on tree	6 - 12
CI6006	Midway Scene (puppet show, arcade, Professor in wagon, midway banner)	10 - 20
CI6007	Midway Scene (fun house, How Strong are You?, Ronald on elephant)	10 - 20
CI6008	Tent Scene (left crowd panel, lion, tiger, Hamburglar)	10 - 20
CI6009	Tent Scene (right crowd panel, Birdie on horse, circus banner)	10 - 20

Boxes

CI6015	Amazing Animal Acts	6 - 12
CI6016	Circus Band	6 - 12
CI6017	Clown Car	6 - 12
CI6018	High Wire Show	6 - 12
CI6019	Monkey Cage	6 - 12
CI6020	Tumblers & Jugglers	6 - 12

Point of Purchase

CI6025	Translite, menu board/drive-thru (large)	10 - 15
CI6026	Message Center Insert, cardboard	8 - 12
CI6027	Permanent Display Header Card	4 - 6

CIRCUS PARADE, 1991

This Mar 8 – Apr 12, 1991 St. Louis regional promotion offered geared action toys (2 vehicles, 2 animals). As each piece moved, parts of the figure also moved. The translite carried just the label of "Circus", while the insert card in each polybag read "Circus Parade." A large circus play surface was created by cutting the sack along the dotted lines and laying it flat.

Premiums

CI6701	Ringmaster Ronald McDonald, Set 1	3 - 6
CI6702	Bareback Rider Birdie, Set 2	3 - 6
CI6703	Elephant Trainer Fry Guy, Set 3	3 - 6
CI6704	Grimace Playing Calliope, Set 4	3 - 6

Sack, 7 " x 13"

| CI6710 | Circus | 1 - 3 |

Point of Purchase

CI6715	Translite, menu board	8 - 12
CI6716	Translite, drive-thru	6 - 10
CI6717	Window Decal	2 - 3

CI6025

CI6715

33

CI6830   CI6831   CI6832

CI6833   CI6834   CI6835

CIRCUS WAGON, 1979

This was the first national Happy Meal promotion and ran June 11 – July 31, 1979. McDonald's selected 6 standard premiums from the K-Promotions catalog to be used. They were pictured on the explanatory material detailing the concept and guidelines for the new offering. An order form was enclosed to be used by all the stores to order these premiums from K-Promotions. Six boxes were designed to look like circus wagons. Character Erasers were the same as those used in Round Top Test II and were designed to fit on top of pencils. These were not issued in polybags. Decals of Big Mac, Hamburglar or Ronald were issued in a polybag with a colored I.D. Bracelet as well as a 60-letter alphabet decal sheet. The Doodler Ruler was placed in a polybag on which the instructions for the placement and use of the *M* circle were printed. Instructions were also printed on the clear polybag containing the tree of Puzzle Lock pieces. The Spinning Top was first used in Round Top Test III. The plastic Wrist Wallet were the same as used in Round Top Test I.

See RO7051   CI6805

Premiums

	Character Erasers – Big Mac, Captain, Hamburglar and Ronald (see RO7051)	
CI6805	I.D. Bracelet – Big Mac, Hamburglar, Ronald (red or yellow)	4 - 10
CI6806	Doodler Ruler – Ronald, 10 different shapes to doodle, 5" ruler and millimeters (red, yellow & blue)	4 - 10
CI6807	Puzzle Lock – Ronald, a lock & puzzle combination, polybagged (red, yellow, & blue)	4 - 10
	Spinning Top (see RO7105)	3 - 4
	Wrist Wallet (see RO7005)	

Boxes

CI6830	Captain/Seal	4 - 8
CI6831	Grimace/Elephant	4 - 8
CI6832	Ronald/Hamburglar/Captain	4 - 8
CI6833	Ronald/Goblins	4 - 8
CI6834	Ronald/Lion	4 - 8
CI6835	Ronald/Mayor McCheese	4 - 8

Point of Purchase

CI6850	Translite, menu board/drive-thru, 6 boxes	10 - 20
CI6851	Translite, menu board/drive-thru, 1 box	10 - 20
CI6852	Ceiling Dangler (see back cover)	40 - 80
CI6853	Floor Display	50 - 90
CI6854	Crew Badge, paper	4 - 5

CI6850

34

CI6806   CI6807

CI6854

C01510

C01511

COLORFORMS, 1986

This Happy Meal national promotion was a tie-in between McDonald's and Colorform playsets from Dec 29, 1986 to Feb 1, 1987. Colorforms had been sold retail for over 30 years. The various plastic shapes on a sheet and the 5" x 5" play scene came polybagged together for each set. A Fry Guy and Fry Girl appeared in every playset, except Grimace's. The 2 "Under 3" premiums used the same Grimace and Ronald character designs, but were <u>sticker</u> playsets rather than Colorforms. The Ronald set came with information printed on the polybag and the Grimace set included information on an insert card.

C01512

Premiums
CO1501	Grimace/Beach, Set 1	2 - 5
CO1502	Hamburglar/Picnic, Set 2	2 - 5
CO1503	Birdie/Playing Outside, Set 3	2 - 5
CO1504	Professor/Camping, Set 4	2 - 5
CO1505	Ronald/Farm, Set 5	2 - 5
CO1506	Grimace/Beach Sticker Set (Under 3)	2 - 7
CO1507	Ronald/Farm Sticker Set (Under 3)	2 - 7

Boxes
CO1510	Beach Party	2 - 4
CO1511	Camp Out	2 - 4
CO1512	Picnic Today!	2 - 4
CO1513	Play Day	2 - 4

Point of Purchase
CO1520	Translite, menu board/drive-thru (large)	6 - 10
CO1521	Translite, drive-thru (small)	4 - 8
CO1522	Message Center Insert, cardboard	6 - 10

C01507

C01506

CO1520

CO1501

CO1502

CO1503

C01513

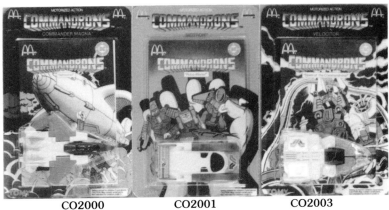

CO1504   CO1505

CO1523 Menu Board Premium Lug-On   6 - 10
CO1525 Translite, drive-thru strip insert   4 - 8

CO2000   CO2001   CO2003

Premiums
CO3200 Birdie on a Tricycle   2 - 5
CO3201 Grimace in a Wagon   2 - 5
CO3202 Hamburglar in an Airplane   2 - 5
CO3203 Ronald McDonald in a Soap-Box Racer 2 - 5

COMMANDRONS, 1985 (unconfirmed)

Four pull back trigger action Commandrons, vehicles which became robots – made by Tomy Corp., were issued in a blister pack bearing the McDonald's logo. There was no McDonald identification on the Commandron. Inside each pack was a small DC comic book, also printed with the McDonald's logo. These were either tested as Happy Meal premiums or as self-liquidator items.

Premiums
CO2000 Commander Magna/ "Airborne!"   – 12
CO2001 Motron/"Robo-Mania"   – 12
CO2002 Solardyn/"The Copy-Bats!"   – 12
CO2003 Velocitor/"Dawn of the Commandrons!" – 12

CONNECTIBLES, 1991

These premiums were given out in the clean-up time after the Barbie/Hot Wheels promotion in Aug/Sept 1991. Stores could order the 4 characters on vehicles and usually received just 1 or 2 characters. The vehicles look like the same as those used in the 1991 Muppet Babies promotion. They can be connected together. No special container or point of purchase displays were available.

CONSTRUX, 1986

The Construx action building system was a tie-in with the Young Astronauts Council for this regional campaign. The snap-together plastic pieces (some of which glowed in the dark) were made by Fisher Price and had a 1986 copyright stamp. A space craft could be assembled by using all 4 sets. Each set was polybagged and came with an instruction sheet and a Happy Meal Proof of Purchase seal. A Construx Alien set could be ordered for 3 seals and $4.50. Two boxes were designed with a space theme.

Premiums
CO3500 Cylinder, Set 1   – 25
CO3501 Canopy, Set 2   – 25
CO3502 Wing, Set 3   – 25
CO3503 Axle, Set 4   – 25
Boxes
CO3510 Computer Quick Fix   6 - 12
CO3511 Marscape   6 - 12
Point of Purchase
CO3515 Translite, menu board   15 - 25
CO3516 Counter Display   150 - 250

CO3200   CO3201   CO3202   CO3203

CO2002

CO3510

CO3500-03, 16

CO3503

CO3501-02

CO5510　　　　　　CO5511

CO3511

CO5512　　　　　　CO5513

CO5504-06

CO5501-03

COSMc CRAYOLA, 1988

McDonald's, Crayola and the Young Astronauts Council shared in producing this Happy Meal. This national promotion ran Apr 15 – May 12, 1988 and featured a new McDonaldland character, CosMc. Each polybagged set included an 8½" x 11" activity space scene provided by the Young Astronauts Council and a different Crayola art medium. The Washable Ink Markers were a new Crayola product and this was the first time chalk had been offered as a Happy Meal premium.

Premiums

CO5501	Crayolas – red, blue, copper, silver – Set 1	2 - 4	
CO5502	Washable Ink Drawing Marker – red – Set 2	2 - 4	
CO5503	Chalk – 4 pastel colors, chalk board – Set 3	2 - 4	
CO5504	Washable Ink Coloring Marker – Set 4	2 - 4	
CO5505	Paint with Water – 3 colors/brush – Set 5	2 - 4	
CO5506	"So Big" – 2 crayons/activity sheet (Under 3)	3 - 5	

Boxes

CO5510	Launch Pad	1 - 3	
CO5511	Lunar Base	1 - 3	
CO5512	Planets	1 - 3	
CO5513	Martians	1 - 3	

Point of Purchase

CO5520	Translite, menu board	6 - 10	
CO5521	Translite, drive-thru	4 - 8	

CR1701 (front)

CR1701

CR1702

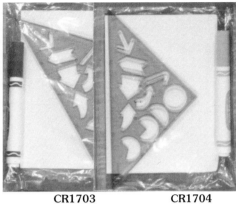
CR1703   CR1704

CR1710   CR1711   CR1735

CO5520

CR1744

CR1740

CRAYOLA, 1986, Test

A Crayola test market was conducted in Evansville, IN in 1986. Various Crayola products were polybagged with plastic stencils having different shaped cut-outs for kids to trace. The triangle stencil/ruler came with a green or orange marker.

Premiums

CR1701	Circle/Compass Stencil (red) w/4 crayons (blue, green, yellow, red)	6 - 10
CR1702	Rectangle Stencil (red) w/4 fluorescent crayons (ultra blue, green, magenta, yellow)	6 - 10
CR1703	Triangle Stencil/Ruler (blue) w/green marker	6 - 12
CR1704	Triangle Stencil/Ruler (blue) w/orange marker	6 - 12

CR1736	CR1737	CR1738

A set in every Happy Meal box.

Set 1   Set 2   Set 3   Set 4

CAUTION: May contain small parts. Not intended for children under 3. Alternate item available on request.

CR1743

CR1729

Boxes

CR1710	Ronald/Grimace Quick Draw	5 - 12
CR1711	Ronald/Ronald Quick Draw	5 - 12

Point of Purchase

CR1715	Translite, menu board	15 - 25

CRAYOLA, 1987

McDonald's and Crayola co-sponsored a "Draw America" contest for kids and an entry form/instruction sheet came in each polybag premium package for this national Happy Meal, Mar 20 – Apr 16, 1987. The graphics on each Happy Meal box were designed to go with a particular stencil. The color band below the Golden Arches handle on each box matched the color of the stencil to be used with it.

Premiums

CR1725	Hamburglar Stencil (orange) w/4 crayons (red, yellow, blue, green), Set 1	2 - 4
CR1726	Birdie Stencil (yellow) w/orange or green thick coloring marker, Set 2	2 - 4
CR1727	Grimace Stencil (purple) w/ 4 fluorescent crayons (ultra yellow, blue, green or hot magenta), Set 3	2 - 4

	CR1810		
		CR1790	

CR1728	Ronald Stencil (red) w/ thin blue or red drawing marker, Set 4	2 - 4
CR1729	Ronald/Fire Truck cardboard stencil w/4 crayons (red, blue, yellow, green) (Under 3)	3 - 5

Boxes

CR1735	Whack Track, orange band	1 - 3
CR1736	Road Maze, yellow band	1 - 3
CR1737	Crazy Face, purple band	1 - 3
CR1738	Absent Apples, red band	1 - 3

Point of Purchase

CR1740	Translite, menu board	6 - 10
CR1741	Translite, drive-thru	4 - 8
CR1742	Message Center Insert, cardboard	6 - 10
CR1743	Menu Board Lug-On w/premiums	12 - 16
CR1744	Counter Mat, plastic	3 - 5

CRAYON SKETCH, 1992

A generic sack began to be used in Jan 1992 as a fill-in between Happy Meals or when supplies of regular boxes were low. The sack was designed as if crayon drawings had been cre-

CR1801	CR1802	CR1803	CR1804

ated with purple, blue, yellow, green colors.

Sack, 6" x 11"
CR1790   Crayon Sketch   1 -3

CRAYON SQUEEZE BOTTLE, 1992

Kay-Bee America's Toy Store and McDonald's produced the Crayon Squeeze Bottle Happy Meal for the New England area during the Open Window (Feb 7 – Mar 6, 1992) period. The premium was a plastic drinking cup with a matching cone top which resembled a crayon when snapped together. Each came with a clear heavy plastic drinking straw and a packet of 3 crayons – red, yellow, blue. The crayons had a RoseArt Brand label and the back of the box was a $1 off coupon on a Kay-Bee purchase. A band of McDonald's *M*s ran around the top and bottom of the cup. The McDonald's name and Kay-Bee American's Toy Store name were printed on opposite sides of the cup. A sack featuring figures to be colored and a $5 off coupon towards any $25+ Kay-Bee purchase were offered.

Premiums
CR1801	Blue	2 - 4
CR1802	Green	2 - 4
CR1803	Red	2 - 4
CR1804	Yellow	2 - 4

Sack, 6" x 12¹/₂"
CR1810	Color the Figures	1 - 4

Point of Purchase
CR1815	Translite, menu board	10 - 12
CR1816	Translite, drive-thru	8 - 10
CR1817	Counter Card	6 - 10

CRAZY CREATURES (Popoids), 1985

This national option Happy Meal ran Aug 2 – Sept 2, 1985 and was a tie-in between McDonald's and Tomy Popoids. Popoids, which can twist, bend and stretch, were introduced in the U.S. in 1983. These were tested in 1984 (see Popoids). Each of the 4 sets contained a connector joint and 2 bellows. The Popoid on the front of the packet was color coded to help employees match them to the correct week. No mention of the Crazy Creatures promotion name was on the package, only on the translite and boxes. Each bag contained a brochure describing the different toys which could be made by connecting various sets. A mail-in coupon and proof-of-purchase was included in the brochure to be used towards the purchase of a Popoids Cosmic Concert musical instrument.

Premiums
CR1950	Column (Wheel) Connector, orange w/10 holes & 2 joints, blue & red (red pkg), Week 1	2 - 6
CR1951	Cube Connector, white w/6 holes & 2 joints, yellow & red (blue pkg), Week 2	2 - 6
CR1952	Ball Connector, white w/6 holes &	2 - 6

CR1965

CR1950	CR1951	CR1952	CR1953

	2 joints, yellow & blue (yellow pkg), Week 3	
CR1953	Pentahedron Connector, orange w/5 holes & 2 joints, yellow & red (white pkg), Week 4	2 - 6

Boxes
CR1960	Elephoid	2 - 5
CR1961	Dragonoids	2 - 5
CR1962	Octopoid	2 - 5
CR1963	Scorpoid	2 - 5

Point of Purchase
CR1965	Translite, menu board/drive-thru (large)	8 - 12
CR1966	Message Center Insert, cardboard	8 - 12
CR1967	Translite, drive-thru strip insert	6 - 8
CR1968	Counter Display w/premiums, motion	60 - 90

CRAZY VEHICLES, 1991

Crazy Vehicles were used as a clean-up premium after the Aug–Sept 91 Barbie/Hot Wheels promotion. Stores were offered these polybagged 3-piece snap-together plastic vehicles

CR1960	CR1961	CR1962

CR1968

CR1963

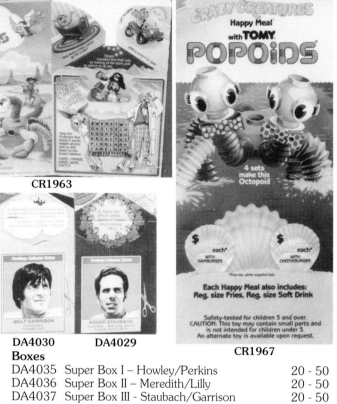

CR1967

and characters with moving wheels, but usually only received 1 or 2 of the characters offered. All premiums could be connected together to form one long vehicle.

Premiums

CR2001	Birdie Airplane, pink	2 - 5
CR2002	Grimace Car, green	2 - 5
CR2003	Hamburglar Train, yellow	2 - 5
CR2004	Ronald McDonald Buggy, red	2 - 5

CR2001   CR2002   CR2003   CR2004

DALLAS COWBOYS, 1980

A 1980 Happy Meal in Dallas featured the Dallas Cowboys football team. The premiums were 6 football trading cards, 2 printed on each of the 3 boxes. Each card featured 1 player.

Premiums

DA4025	Chuck Howley	6 - 10
DA4026	Don Perkins	6 - 10
DA4027	Don Meredith	6 - 10
DA4028	Bob Lilly	6 - 10
DA4029	Roger Staubach	6 - 10
DA4030	Walt Garrison	6 - 10

DA4030   DA4029

Boxes

DA4035	Super Box I – Howley/Perkins	20 - 50
DA4036	Super Box II – Meredith/Lilly	20 - 50
DA4037	Super Box III - Staubach/Garrison	20 - 50

DAY & NIGHT, 1985

Two generic cartons were made available in 1985 for stores to use when they ran out of regular Happy Meal boxes. No premiums were produced for these boxes.

Boxes

DA8025	All-Star Sunday	2 - 4
DA8026	Who's Afraid of the Dark?	2 - 4

DA4025-26

DA4036 (DA4027)   DA4036 (back-DA4028)

DA8025-26

41

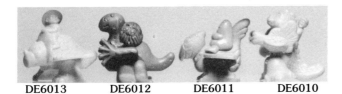

| DE6013 | DE6012 | DE6011 | DE6010 |

DESIGN–O–SAURS, 1987

Design-O-Saurs, only in the colors listed below, were offered to stores for use as premiums, July 10 – Aug 6, 1987. These were used on a limited regional basis. There were no containers. Some stores ordered these later for give-aways. The plastic snap-together 5-piece toys came on a tree. The supply company offering the Design-O-Saurs recommended 2 alternate premiums for "Under 3" usage and later produced the Design–O–Saurs in different colors.

Premiums

DE6010	Ronald on a Tyrannosaurus Rex, red, Week 1	3 - 5
DE6011	Grimace on a Pterodactyl, purple, Week 2	3 - 5
DE6012	Fry Guy on a Brontosaurus, green, Week 3	3 - 5
DE6013	Hamburglar on a Triceratops, orange, Week 4	3 - 5
	Fry Guy Happy Car (see LI3405)	
	Grimace Happy Taxi (see LI3406)	

Point of Purchase

| DE6020 | Translite, menu board | 10 - 14 |
| DE6021 | Translite, drive-thru | 8 - 10 |

DINK THE LITTLE DINOSAUR, 1990

A Saturday morning cartoon series provided the characters for this regional Happy Meal, Aug 1990. It was a 2-week promotion in OK and TX. Dink was copyrighted by Ruby Spears, Inc. The 6 characters came polybagged with a diorama paper scene to back-up the character. Interesting information about each character was printed on the back of the diorama.

| | | | DI1104 | DI1103 |
| DI1102 | DI1105 | DI1101 | DI1100 |

DI1115

Premiums

DI1100	Crusty, giant sea turtle, green, Set 1	3 - 8
DI1101	Amber, corythosaurus, beige, Set 2	3 - 8
DI1102	Scat, compsognalthus, green, Set 3	3 - 8
DI1103	Shyler, edaphosaurus, green, Set 4	3 - 8
DI1104	Flapper, pterodon, brown, Set 5	3 - 8
DI1105	Dink, apatasaurus, green, Set 6	3 - 8

Box

| DI1110 | Dink | 1 - 3 |

Point of Purchase

| DI1115 | Translite, menu board | 8 - 12 |
| DI1116 | Translite, drive-thru | 6 - 8 |

DI1110

DINOSAUR DAYS, 1981/82

Dinosaur Days was a national option Happy Meal, Oct 5, '81 to Jan 24, '82. The McDonald's corporation designed six boxes for this promotion, but regions developed their own premiums or purchased generic ones from McDonald's suppliers.

Suggested items from M-B Sales included: Dinosaur Sponge; Ronald Sponge; Grimace Sponge; Birdie Sponge; Ronald Flying Wheel; McDonaldland Tic–Tac–Top; Ronald Denim Look Pocket Patch; Ronald Nose Maze Game; Ronald Whistle Ring; Ronald Very, Very, Very Long Whistle; Grimace Very, Very, Very Long Whistle; Ronald & Grimace Glow Rings; Ronald & Grimace Forks and Spoons; McDonaldland Character Face Magnets; Ronald & Grimace Combs; Ronald & Grimace Fun Mold.

Some areas used Diener dinosaur figures or X-O graph cards. The Diener figures came in brown, gray, green, orange and blue with possible other colors being used. The 6 X-O graph cards measured $2^1/_2$" x 2" and contained text by the Editors of *World Book Encyclopedia* on the reverse side of the print. They also carried the McDonald's Corporation 1981 copyright.

| DI1202 | DI1205 | DI1201 | DI1203 | DI1200 | DI1204 |

Premiums

DI1200	Ankylosaurus Diener figure	1 - 3
DI1201	Dimetrodon Diener figure	1 - 3
DI1202	Pteranodon Diener figure	1 - 3
DI1203	Stegosaurus Diener figure	1 - 3
DI1204	Triceratops Diener figure	1 - 3
DI1205	Tyrannosaurus Rex Diener figure	1 - 3
DI1206	Mastodons X-O graph, #1	6 - 12
DI1207	Stegosaurus X-O graph, #2	6 - 12
DI1208	Triceratops X-O graph, #3	6 - 12
DI1209	Brontosaurus X-O graph, #4	6 - 12
DI1210	Saber-Toothed Tiger X-O graph, #5	6 - 12
DI1211	Tyrannosaurus Rex X-O graph, #6	6 - 12
DI1212	Dinosaur Sponge, McDonald's logo charm hanging around neck	2 - 6

| DI1206 | DI1207 | DI1208 | DI1209 | DI1210 | DI1211 |

| DI1225 | DI1226 | DI1227 |

| DI1228 | DI1229 | DI1230 |

DI1235

Point of Purchase

DI1235   Translite, menu board/drive-thru (large)   10 - 20

DINOSAURS (Talking Storybook), 1989

Storybooks with cassette tapes featuring Bones, a 3-year old brontosaurus, and Dodo, a 3-year old pterodactyl, were the premiums in a MI and WI Happy Meal offered during the summer of 1989. The stories were written by Mark Saltzman and Pat Collins and were copyrighted by Music Publishing International. Children could read the book as they listened to the tape. Each 16-page book measured 6" x 5" and came polybagged with a matching colored tape. The translite designation read "Dinosaur Happy Meal"; the sack claimed "Talking Storybook Happy Meal".

Premiums

DI1300   Amazing Birthday Adventure, yellow   4 - 8
DI1301   Creature in the Cave, purple   4 - 8

Boxes

DI1225	Anatosaurus	10 - 18
DI1226	Ankylosaurus	10 - 18
DI1227	Brachrosaurus	10 - 18
DI1228	Brontosaurus	10 - 18
DI1229	Three Skeletons	10 - 18
DI1230	Woolly Mammoth	10 - 18

DI1212

DI1303   DI1300

DI1310

DI3030

DI3027   DI3026

	book (blue), 3-toed sloth punch-out, Week 3		
DI3028	Wonders in the Wild – 16-pg activity book (tan), butterfly punch-out, Week 4	1 - 3	

Sack

DI3030	Discover	1 - 2

Point of Purchase

DI3035	Translite, menu-board	6 - 10
DI3036	Translite, drive-thru	4 - 8

DISNEY FAVORITES, 1987

Four Walt Disney movie classics were featured in the Disney Favorites Happy Meals, Nov 30 – Dec 24, 1987. This was the first Disney-related Happy Meal. Four activity books, created exclusively for McDonald's by Western Publishing Co., included coupon advertisements for Disney-related products. Two boxes were designed for the promotion, each included one scene from each of the four films.

DI3301   DI3302

DI3303   DI3300

Premiums

DI3300	*Cinderella* Paint with Water book, 8" x 10¹/₄", 32 pgs (paint printed "in" the paper & activated by a wet paint brush), Week 1	1 - 5
DI3301	*Lady and the Tramp* sticker activity book, 8" x 8", 12 pgs, Week 2	1 - 5
DI3302	*Dumbo* press-out book, 8" x 8", 12 pgs, Week 3	1 - 5
DI3303	*The Sword in the Stone* activity book, 8" x 11", 32 pgs, Week 4	1 - 5

DI1301   DI1302

DI1302	Danger Under the Lake, blue–green	4 - 8
DI1303	Dinosaur Baby Boom, pink	4 - 8

Sack, 8¹/₂" x 12"

DI1310	Bones & Dodo, white	1 - 3

Point of Purchase

DI1315	Translite, menu board	8 - 12
DI1316	Translite, drive-thru	6 - 8

DISCOVER THE RAIN FOREST, 1991

Teaching kids about the environment highlighted the Rain Forest Happy Meal, Sept 6 – Oct 3, 1991. Each of the 4 books contained a letter expressing concern for Rain Forest preservation from McDonald's and Conservation International. The 7" x 8", full color books were printed on recycled stock and developed exclusively for this national promotion.

DI3028   DI3025

Premiums

DI3025	Sticker Safari – 12-pg sticker & activity book (green), w/14 reusable animal stickers, full page punch-out of a Toucan, Week 1	1 - 3
DI3026	Paint It Wild – 16-pg paint & activity book (purple), 12 different 5 water color paint pallets, tree frog punch-out, Week 2	1 - 3
DI3027	Jewel of the Amazon Kingdom – 16-pg story-	1 - 3

DI3322

DU1004   DU1002   DU1003   DU1001   DU1005

DI3320

DI3310   DI3311   DU1010

Boxes		
DI3310	Cinderella/Godmother	1 - 3
DI3311	Cinderella/Prince	1 - 3
Point of Purchase		
DI3320	Translite, menu board	6 - 10
DI3321	Translite, drive-thru	4 - 8
DI3322	Menu Board Premium Lug-On	6 - 10

Point of Purchase		
DU1020	Translite, menu board	6 - 10
DU1021	Translite, drive-thru	4 - 8

DUCK TALES I, 1988

"Duck Tales" was a weekday afternoon TV series for kids produced by Walt Disney Studios. The adventure series starred Scrooge McDuck and his nephews: Huey, Louie and Dewey. This national promotion ran Feb 5 – Mar 10, 1988. Only the "Under 3" premium came in a polybag.

Premiums		
DU1001	Duck Code Quacker, orange	1 - 3
DU1002	Magnifying Glass, green	1 - 3
DU1003	Telescope, yellow w/either a horizontal or vertical decal	1 - 3
DU1004	Wrist–Wallet Decoder, blue, 2-pcs on tree	1 - 3
DU1005	Magic Motion Map & decoder (Under 3)	2 - 4
Boxes		
DU1010	City of Gold	1 - 3
DU1011	Cookie of Fortune	1 - 3
DU1012	Hula Hoopla!	1 - 3
DU1013	Westward Dough!	1 - 3

DU1020

| DU1011 | DU1012 | DU1013 |

DUCK TALES II, 1988

A regional (TX and MI) Happy Meal in 1988 featured Duck Tales again, but this time with characters in vehicles. The regular meal premiums were of 2-piece construction with moving wheels, while the "Under 3" premium was a 1-piece figure.

Premiums

DU1030	Scrooge McDuck in car, red, Set 1	3 - 6
DU1031	Webby on tricycle, blue, Set 2	3 - 6
DU1032	Launchpad in airplane, orange, Set 3	3 - 6
DU1033	Huey, Dewey & Louie on surf ski, green/ yellow, Set 4	3 - 6
DU1034	Huey Skating (Under 3)	3 - 8

| DU1031 | DU1032 | DU1033 | DU1030 | DU1034 |

DU1040

Box

DU1040	Duck Tales press-outs	2 - 4

Point of Purchase

DU1045	Translite, menu board	8 - 12
DU1046	Translite, drive-thru	6 - 10

DUKES OF HAZZARD, 1982

The CBS TV series "Dukes of Hazzard" was the inspiration for this regional Happy Meal which ran for 6 weeks in 1982 (May 21 – July 4). It is known to have been done in NE, NC, Kansas City and the St. Louis region. The 3-piece plastic vehicles with decals served as the Happy Meal containers as well. "Dukes of Hazzard" character cups were also a part of the promotion in some areas. These could be purchased for a small up-charge with the order of a medium or large soft drink or with the Happy Meal.

DU1045

| DU1212 | DU1215 | DU1213 | DU1214 | DU1211 | DU1210 |

Premiums

DU1200	General Lee, orange, Weeks 1 and 6	10 - 20
DU1201	Boss Hogg Cadillac, white, Week 2	10 - 20
DU1202	Sheriff Roscoe Car, white, Week 3	10 - 20
DU1203	Daisy's Jeep, white, Week 4	10 - 20
DU1204	Uncle Jesse's Pick-Up Truck, white, Week 5	10 - 20
DU1205	DU1200-04, vehicle w/o stickers	5 - 10
DU1206	DU1200-04, vehicle & separate sticker sheet	15 - 25
DU1207	DU1200-04, sticker sheet only	8 - 10
DU1210	Luke character cup, Week 1	2 - 4
DU1211	Boss Hogg character cup, Week 2	2 - 4
DU1212	Sheriff Roscoe & dog, Flash character cup, Week 3	2 - 4
DU1213	Daisy character cup, Week 4	2 - 4
DU1214	Uncle Jesse character cup, Week 5	2 - 4
DU1215	Bo character cup, Week 6	2 - 4

Point of Purchase

DU1225	Translite (cars), menu board/drive-thru (large)	10 - 20
DU1226	Translite (cups), menu board/drive-thru (lg)	10 - 20

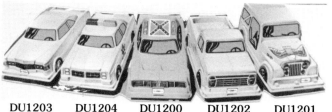

DU1203   DU1204   DU1200   DU1202   DU1201

DU1227

ET7010

DU1228

DU1225

E.T. POSTERS
One with every McDonald's Happy Meal

ET7000   ET7002   ET7003

DU1227 Ceiling Dangler, cars   60 - 100
DU1228 Floor Display, Boss Hogg, 4' high   15 - 30

NEW POSTER EACH WEEK
COLLECT ALL FOUR!
ALL ROYALTIES BENEFIT THE SPECIAL OLYMPICS

ET7024

E.T., 1985

E.T., The Extra Terrestrial was first released by director Steven Spielberg and Universal Studios in June of 1982. This Happy Meal tied-in with the re-release of the movie in July 1985. The promotion ran from July 5 to Aug 1 and all royalties paid by McDonald's were donated to the Special Olympics. The 4-color posters measured 17" x 24" and had to be hand rolled by the employees and secured with a rubber band as they would not fit into the box. The box design was changed to accommodate the 6-piece McNuggets carton.

Premiums
ET7000   E.T./Bike   4 - 8

ET7001	E.T./Boy/Girl	4 - 8
ET7002	E.T./Glowing Finger	4 - 8
ET7003	E.T./Radio Device	4 - 8
Boxes		
ET7010	E.T. Makes Friends	2 - 4
ET7011	The Great Adventure	2 - 4
Point of Purchase		
ET7020	Translite, menu board, motion wheel	10 - 15
ET7021	Translite, drive-thru (large)	8 - 12
ET7022	Translite, drive-thru (small)	6 - 8
ET7023	Menu Board Lug-On	10 - 15
ET7024	Wall Display (This Week's Poster)	10 - 15

| ET7025 | Message Center Insert | 8 - 10 |
| ET7026 | Permanent Display Header Card | 4 - 6 |

| ET7011 | ET7001 |

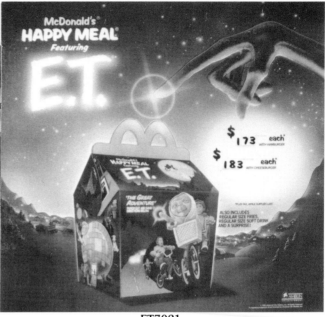

ET7021

FEELING GOOD, 1985

The national Feeling Good Happy Meal promotion ran for 10 weeks from Dec 26, 1985 to Mar 9, 1986. It coincided with National Dental Health month in Feb 1986. All the premiums were health related items and the 4 boxes were printed with tips on good health habits plus jokes and puzzles. Only the 2 toothbrushes and the mirror came in polybags.

| FE1002 | FE1001 |

Premiums
FE1001	Ronald Toothbrush, white/red	3 - 6
FE1002	Hamburglar Toothbrush, white/black	3 - 6
FE1003	Grimace Soap Dish, purple	2 - 4
FE1004	Fry Guy Sponge, green	2 - 4
FE1005	Birdie Mirror, yellow	2 - 6
FE1006	The Captain Comb, red	2 - 4
	Grimace Tub Toy (see SH5054)	
	Fry Guy & Friend Tub Toy (see SH5055)	

Boxes
FE1015	Child in Mirror	2 - 4
FE1016	Hidden Toothbrushes	2 - 4
FE1017	Characters Warm-Up	2 - 4
FE1018	Reverse Message	2 - 4

FE1025

| FE1004 | FE1003 | FE1006 | FE1005 |

| FE1015 | FE1016 | FE1017 |

48

E.T. POSTERS
One with every McDonald's Happy Meal

THIS WEEK'S POSTER

E.T.

NEW POSTER EACH WEEK
COLLECT ALL FOUR!
ALL ROYALTIES BENEFIT THE SPECIAL OLYMPICS

RONALD McDONALD and HIS FRIENDS

COLLECT ALL 6
ONE FREE PER VISIT TO CHILDREN 12 AND UNDER

McDonald's
Super Summer

McDonald's
Super Summer
HAPPY MEAL
COLLECT ALL 5!

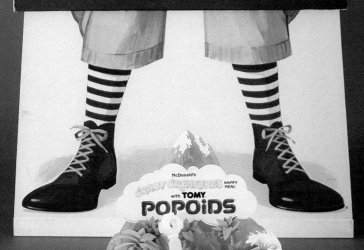

McDonald's CRAZY CREATURES HAPPY MEAL
with TOMY
POPOIDS

Three-piece set in every box!

COLLECT ALL 4 SETS AND BOXES
TO MAKE OODLES OF CREATURES!

COWPOKE   FIRST-CLASS   SARGE   DRUMMER   CORNY   SPARKY   BOOMERANG   VOLLEY   SNORKEL   ROCKER

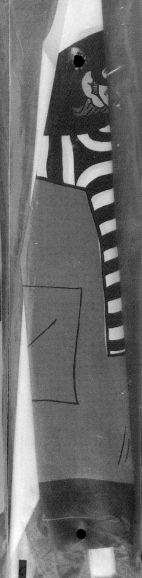

Food and Fun in a Box

HAPPY MEAL

$1.30 EACH

McDonald's

HAPPY MEAL

Presenting
THE ADVENTURES OF
Ronald McDonald
HAPPY MEAL
COLLECT ALL SIX ADVENTURES.
A PRIZE IN EVERY BOX!

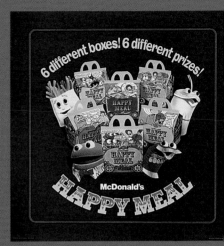

6 different boxes! 6 different prizes!

McDonald's

HAPPY MEAL

McDonald's
ASTROSNIKS
HAPPY MEAL

Get one AstroSnik in every Happy Meal.

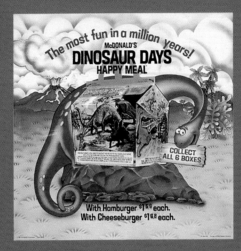

The most fun in a million years!

McDONALD'S
DINOSAUR DAYS
HAPPY MEAL

COLLECT ALL 6 BOXES

With Hamburger $1.59 each.
With Cheeseburger $1.68 each.

undersea
Happy Meal
has surfaced!

Happy Meal

6 New Boxes and a Prize in every box!

NOW McDONALD'S HAS A FARM
Collect a Playmates Farm Friend
with every Barnyard Happy Meal.

Playmates

SPACE
ALIENS

Get one free in every Happy Meal.

The best time you can have
with your glasses on.

3-D HAPPY MEAL

Collect all 4

Out of this world.
Unidentified Happy Meal.

collect them all

McDonald's
DINOSAURS
Happy Meal

Collect all 8!
Delightful, colorful little creatures from the
magical Isle of Tiny. There's one in every Happy Meal.

McDonald's
STAR TREK
MEAL

FE1018	FL4010	FR1130

Point of Purchase

FE1025	Translite, menu board/drive-thru (large)	8 - 10
FE1026	Translite, drive-thru (small)	6 - 8
FE1027	Message Center Insert	6 - 10
FE1028	Menu Board Lug-On	6 - 10

FLINTSTONE KIDS, 1988

This 1988 regional Happy Meal (New England and FL) featured the Hanna–Barbera Flintstone Kids. Each removable figure came with a vehicle with moving wheels. The "Under 3" premium was a 1-piece construction. Each came in a polybag with an insert card.

Premiums

FL4001	Barney/Mastodon mobile, blue	4 - 10
FL4002	Betty/Pterydactil mobile, orange	4 - 10

in the Bluefield-Beckley and Charleston-Huntington, WV areas. Each of the 4 characters in a vehicle was polybagged and came with a description card with a cave like border. Sets 2 and 4 were not carried over when this promotion went national.

Premiums

FR1100	Gobo Fraggle in orange carrot, wheel offset to make it wobble (wheels larger for national offer), Set 1	15 - 20
FR1101	Bulldoozer and Friends, gray, black, yellow, Set 2	15 - 20
FR1102	Red Fraggle in Radish, green, wheels offset (wheels larger for national offer), Set 3	15 - 20
FR1103	Cotterpin Doozer and Friends, gray, black, yellow, Set 4	15 - 20

Box

FR1108	Fraggle Rock	10 - 20

FL4002	FL4001	FL4003	FL4004	FL4005	FR1100	FR1101	FR1102	FR1103	

FL4003	Fred/Gator mobile, green	4 - 10
FL4004	Wilma/Dragon mobile, purple	4 - 10
FL4005	Dino figure, purple (Under 3)	4 - 13

Box

FL4010	Drive in Country	5 - 10

Point of Purchase

FL4015	Translite, menu board	10 - 20

FRAGGLE ROCK, 1987, Test

This Apr 24 – May 28, 1987 promotion was test marketed

FRAGGLE ROCK, 1988

Jim Henson's *Fraggle Rock* Saturday morning cartoon series began in the fall of 1987 on NBC. The national tie-in Happy Meal ran Mar 11 – Apr 7, 1988. The 2-piece premiums featured the 4 characters in vegetable vehicles and were polybagged with an insert card. The "Under 3" offer was a 1-piece character with no vehicle.

Premiums

FR1120	Gobo in his carrot, orange, Set 1	1 - 3
FR1121	Red in her radish, red, Set 2	1 - 3

FR1131	FR1132	FR1133

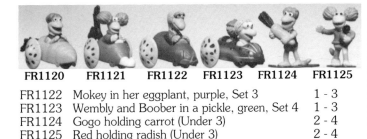

FR1120	FR1121	FR1122
FR1123	FR1124	FR1125

FR1122	Mokey in her eggplant, purple, Set 3	1 - 3
FR1123	Wembly and Boober in a pickle, green, Set 4	1 - 3
FR1124	Gogo holding carrot (Under 3)	2 - 4
FR1125	Red holding radish (Under 3)	2 - 4

Boxes

FR1130	Radish Tops	1 - 3

FR1131	Party Picks	1 - 3
FR1132	Radishes in Cave	1 - 3
FR1133	Swimming Hole Blues	1 - 3

Point of Purchase

FR1140	Translite, menu board	6 - 10
FR1141	Translite, drive-thru	4 - 8
FR1142	Dangler, 1 for each premium, each	2 - 4
FR1143	Counter Display w/premiums	50 - 75
FR1144	Register Topper	2 - 4
FR1145	Crew Button	1 - 2

FRIENDLY SKIES, 1991

Full-page newspaper ads in Oct, 1991 announced the Friendly Skies Meal from United Airlines and McDonald's. By notifying the airlines 6 hours before departure on flights to and from Orlando, FL, this special service could be reserved. Food offerings included: a sausage biscuit, fruit and milk; a cheeseburger or fajita, carrot sticks, cookie, and milk; for snack flights: a peanut butter and jelly sandwich, milk. Although macaroni and cheese was listed, it was not available.

The first toy was to have been Ronald in a United plane, but these were not available until well after Oct 31, so several other McDonald toys were given out. In early 1992, the 1-piece action toys of Ronald and Grimace were ready. Each toy came in a printed polybag with McDonald's and United "wing" logos.

The "game boxes" were specially designed to fit on airline food carts. Two sizes have been located: $6^{1}/_{2}$" x $6^{1}/_{2}$"x $3^{1}/_{4}$" and $5^{1}/_{4}$" x $5^{1}/_{4}$" x $2^{1}/_{2}$". Although the graphics were the same on each box, the smaller size had printing on the center leg of the stylized *M* handle to indicate which toy was included.

A packet containing 2 colored pencils, a straw, moist towelette and napkin was also included in each box.

Premiums

FR1301	Ronald	6 - 12
FR1302	Grimace	6 - 12

Boxes

FR1310	Larger box, no indication of toy	4 - 6
FR1311	Smaller box, Ronald or Grimace toy notice	4 - 6
FR1312	Napkin Packet	2 - 3

FR1140

FR1302   FR1301

FR1143

FR1311 (Grimace)   FR1311 (Ronald)   FR1311 - *back*

FR1501

FR1502

FR1510

FROM THE HEART, 1990

McDonaldland characters appeared on 2 different sets of valentine cards during the 13-day national option promotion of Feb 2–14, 1990. Each set consisted of 6 scratch and sniff cards (one set was chocolate scented; the other cinnamon). The cards were polybagged and came attached to each other to be torn apart. A "To/From" notation was on the reverse side. The box was designed to serve as a mailbox.

Premiums

FR1501	Ronald Frosting Cake, chocolate scent	1 - 4
FR1502	Ronald/Hot Chocolate, cinnamon scent	1 - 4

Box

FR1510	Play Matchmaker	1 - 3

Point of Purchase

FR1515	Translite, menu board	8 - 10
FR1516	Translite, drive-thru	6 - 8

FR2002   FR2001   FR2003   FR2004   FR2005

FR1312   FR2010

FR1515

FRY BENDERS, 1990

French fries which made into characters provided the premiums for this MI regional Happy Meal, Sept 7 – Oct 4, 1990. It later ran in other regions. Each bendable fry in a sporting activity came in 3 interchangeable pieces – body, arms and feet. The "Under 3" figure was a single piece.

Premiums

FR2001	Freestyle the Roller Skater	3 - 5
FR2002	Froggy the Scuba Diver	3 - 5
FR2003	Grand Slam the Baseball Player	3 - 5

FR2015

FU5007   FU5008   FU5009

FU5010

FU5000   FU5001   FU5002   FU5003

FR2004	Roadie the Bicycler, turnable wheels	3 - 5
Box		
FR2010	Fry Bender Cut-Outs	1 - 3
Point of Purchase		
FR2015	Translite, menu board	8 - 12
FR2016	Translite, drive-thru	6 - 8

| FR2005 | Tunes on a skateboard/jam box (Under 3) | 4 - 6 |

FUN WITH FOOD, 1989

Fun With Food was a tie-in with the release of the Fisher-Price/McDonald's Fun With Food retail line. This national option Happy Meal ran Sept 1 – 28, 1989. Fisher-Price made one child-size McDonald's restaurant available to each store as a drawing sweepstakes prize. The 4 unique play food items (with a decal sheet) were available only at McDonald's. Each polybag included a Fun With Food line flyer.

Premiums

FU5000	Hamburger Guy, 3 pcs, #1	2 - 6
FU5001	French Fry Guy, 3 pcs, #2	2 - 6
FU5002	Soft Drink Guy, 2 pcs, #3	2 - 6
FU5003	Chicken McNugget Guys, 4 pcs, #4	2 - 6
Boxes		
FU5007	3-Ring Circus	1 - 3
FU5008	In Concert	1 - 3
FU5009	Making a Splash	1 - 3
FU5010	Movie Making	1 - 3
Point of Purchase		
FU5015	Translite, menu board	6 - 10
FU5016	Translite, drive-thru	4 - 8

FU5015

FUNNY FRY FRIENDS, 1989

The back of the 1989 dated insert card within the polybag stated "Collect all 4". It is not known if these were from a test or if they were packaged as a clean-up toy. Some of the premiums were given out during clean-up times in MD and PA in May 1991.

Premiums

FU5200	Gadzooks, Groucho-type character, 3 pcs	– – 15
FU5201	Matey, pirate, 3 pcs	– – 15
FU5202	Tracker, explorer, 3 pcs	– – 15
FU5203	ZZZ's, sleepy Fry Guy, 3 pcs	– – 15

FUNNY FRY FRIENDS, 1990

The McDonaldland Fry Kids characters became Funny Fry Friends for this national Happy Meal which ran Dec 22, 1989 to Jan 18, 1990. Each character had 3 parts (body, legs, headgear) which were interchangeable with others in the series. Each polybag contained an insert card which read "Collect all 8". Some packages came with a $3 bonus book of coupons to be used for savings on brand name products. The "Under 3" figures were of 1-piece construction.

Premiums

FU5210	Hoops, basketball player, #1	2 - 4
FU5211	Rollin' Rocker, roller skater/headphones, #2	2 - 4
FU5212	Gadzooks (same as FU5200), #3	2 - 4
FU5213	Matey (same as FU5201), #4	2 - 4

| FU5200 | FU5202 | FU5203 | | | | | | | FU5225 |

FU5210 FU5211 FU5213 FU5212 FU5214 FU5215 FU5216 FU5217 FU5219 FU5218

FU5226   FU5227   FU5228

FU5235

FU5237

FU5214	Tracker (same as FU5202), #5	2 - 4
FU5215	ZZZ's (same as FU5203), #6	2 - 4
FU5216	Too Tall, clown on stilts, #7	2 - 4
FU5217	Sweet Cuddles, baby Fry Girl, #8	2 - 4
FU5218	Little Darling, cow girl (Under 3)	3 - 6
FU5219	Lil' Chief, Indian (Under 3)	3 - 6

Boxes

FU5225	Cool Day at School	1 - 3
FU5226	City Sights	1 - 3
FU5227	Ski Holiday	1 - 3
FU5228	Snowy Day Play	1 - 3

Point of Purchase

FU5235	Translite, menu board	6 - 10
FU5236	Translite, drive-thru	4 - 8
FU5237	Counter Display, battery operated	60 - 90

61

FUN–TO–GO, 1977

In 1977, Dick Brams, McDonald's St. Louis regional advertising manager, asked 2 advertising agencies to help develop a meal for kids. A Kansas City agency proposed their idea as a "Happy Meal". The St. Louis agency (Stolz) suggested a "Fun-to-Go" meal. This meal would feature a regular hamburger or cheeseburger, fries, McDonaldland cookie samples and a premium with a Fun-to-Go box – it did not include a drink. Suggested pricing was 95¢ for the hamburger meal and $1.05 for the cheeseburger meal. This test promotion ran from 10/17/77 to 10/16/78 and utilized generic premiums which did not fit the theme of the boxes produced. Each of the 6 boxes measured 2" x 8" x 8³/₄" including the handle.

Peel-off bike fender stickers featured the McDonald characters: Big Mac (red), Captain (orange), Hamburglar (blue), and Ronald (green). Each one measured 2¹/₄" x 3¹/₂" and came in a polybag.

Six water color swatches were across the top of the folded Color-Card. These were to be used to paint a picture of the character and the scene printed on the rest of the card. These were sealed in a polybag.

Faces of McDonaldland characters became the main piece in the 3" x 3¹/₄" paper Create-A-Face premium. Two perforated strips – one printed with 2–3 eye variations; the other, mouth configurations – were to be separated and inserted into the slots in the face to create funny faces. Issued in a polybag.

A specially treated picture was utilized for the Fortune Burger. Rubbing the hamburger portion of the sandwich with a wet cloth would reveal 1 of the 12 printed fortunes. This cardboard piece measured 3¹/₂" x 2"and came in a polybag.

Iron-on color designs of McDonald characters were presented in the Heat Transfers. Each transfer measured 2¹/₂" x 3" and were also polybagged.

Heads of McDonaldland characters became the oversized middle portion of 8" plastic straws. These came in green, yellow, red, or blue and were polybagged.

Space Raiders were soft rubber premiums made by the Diener Co. Four space ships and 4 space raiders were offered.

The name of each ship or raider was molded into the piece. Each came in blue, green, orange, pink and yellow. Diener also sold these in retail stores.

Stencil-A-Face premiums required perforated areas to be punched out of each stencil. One could draw the head outline of a McDonald character by using both sides of the stencil; then the eyes, nose and mouth could be traced into position. Different expressions could be created by using different sets of features. Each polybagged stencil measured 3¹/₄" x 3¹/₄".

Premiums

FU7001	Bike Fender Sticker – Big Mac (7001), Captain (7002), Hamburglar (7003), Ronald (7004)	5 - 10
FU7005	Color-Card – Captain (7005), Fry Goblins (7006), Hamburglar (7007), Ronald (7008)	5 - 10
FU7009	Create-A-Face – Grimace (7009),	5 - 10

FU7001   FU7002   FU7003   FU7004

FU7005   FU7011   FU7009

FU7035

FU7036

FU7037

FU7037 - back

FU7039

FU7040

FU7013

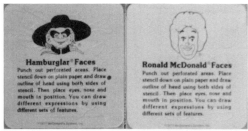

FU7030   **FU7031**

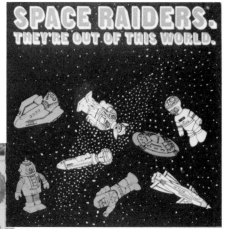

FU7047

FU7026 FU7027 FU7028 FU7029 FU7022 FU7024 FU7023 FU7025

FU7016   **FU7014**

	Hamburglar (7010), Mayor (7011), Ronald (7012)		
FU7013	Fortune Burger, 12 different fortunes,	5 - 10	
FU7014	Heat Transfer – Fry Goblins (7014), Grimace (7015), Mayor (7016), Ronald (7017)	5 - 10	
FU7018	McDonaldland Character Straws – Big Mac (7018), Grimace (7019), Hamburglar (7020), Ronald (7021)	5 - 10	
FU7022	Space Raiders – Brak (7022), Dard (7023), Horta (7024), Zama (7025) Space Ships: Altair (7026), Ceti-3 (7027), Lyra (7028), Krygo 5 (7029)	50¢ - 1	
FU7030	Stencil-A-Face – Hamburglar (7030), Ronald (7031)	5 - 10	

Boxes

FU7035	Filet-o-Fantasy, #1	30 - 50
FU7036	The Professor in His Laboratory/ Shake a Pickle, #2	30 - 50
FU7037	Planet of the Pickles/The Maze Craze, #3	30 - 50
FU7038	McMobile, #4	30 - 50
FU7039	McDonald's Restaurant/Breakfast, #5	30 - 50
FU7040	Big Burger Country, #6	30 - 50

Point of Purchase

FU7045	Translite, Fun-To-Go	20 - 30
FU7046	Translite, Space Raiders	15 - 25
FU7047	Register Topper, Space Raiders	8 - 12
FU7048	Ceiling Dangler, Space Raiders	20 - 30

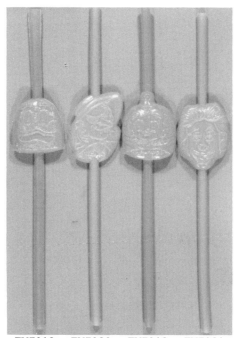

FU7019   FU7020   FU7018   FU7021

GA5503	Garfield on scooter, big smile, gray vest, yellow handlebars on red scooter w/green wheels	10 -2 0
GA5504	Garfield in car, purple hat, purple neck scarf, dark blue car w/yellow trim and tires	10 - 20

GA5501   GA5503   GA5504   GA5502

GARFIELD, 1988, Test

Garfield, created by Jim Davis, has had a show on Saturday morning TV on CBS and is a comic strip star. In July 1988, he was featured in a McDonald's test Happy Meal promotion in the Charleston, SC and Erie, PA areas. A removeable Garfield came with 4 different means of transportation. Each came in a polybag with a 1-color insert card. No "Under 3" premiums, boxes or point of purchase materials have been identified.

Premiums

GA5501	Garfield on skateboard, pink helmet (no straps), white flowered shirt, hot pink skateboard, 6-spoke green wheels	10 - 20
GA5502	Garfield on a Big Wheel tricycle, yellow cap on backwards, blue overalls, green tricycle w/purple wheels	10 - 20

GARFIELD, 1989

From June 23 – July 20, 1989 Garfield was the leading character in a McDonald's national Happy Meal promotion. Four removeable posed figures in 4 unique vehicles were used as premiums in the regular meals. Naturally the "Under 3" premium was a 1-piece design. Some premiums came in a polybag with an insert card; others in a polybag with the descriptive information printed on the bag. Four boxes were used nationally, with a 4-color Safari Garfield sack being test marketed in one region.

Premiums

GA6001	Garfield on scooter, yellow, Set 1	1 - 3
GA6002	Garfield in 4-wheeler, blue, Set 2	1 - 3
GA6003	Garfield on skateboard, pink, Set 3	1 - 3
GA6004	Garfield on motorcycle with Odie (not removeable) inside car, red, Set 4	1 - 3

GA6010 GA6011 GA6012

GA6013

GA6014

GA6022

GA6001 GA6002 GA6003 GA6004 GA6005 GA6006

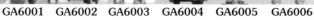

GA6020

GA6005	Garfield on roller skates (Under 3)	3 - 5
GA6006	Garfield with Pooky on skateboard (Under 3)	3 - 5
Boxes/Sack		
GA6010	AHH, Vacation!!!	1 - 3
GA6011	Cat with a Mission	1 - 3
GA6012	Garfield Catches Lunch	1 - 3
GA6013	Mischief This Morning	1 - 3
GA6014	Safari Garfield (sack)	6 - 10
Point of Purchase		
GA6020	Translite, menu board	6 - 10
GA6021	Translite, drive-thru	4 - 8
GA6022	Counter Display w/premiums	50 - 80
GA6023	Dangler, 1 for each premium, each	3 - 6

GENERIC (Happy Meal Test IV), 1979

Testing continued in the first half of 1979, leading up to the first national Happy Meal (see Circus Wagon, 1979). At this point in the test, the "round top" box was discontinued. Five boxes were designed such that the handle no longer fit through a slot, thus making them easier for the crew to assemble. Areas taking part in this portion of the test were Kansas City; St. Louis; Denver; Buffalo and Albany, NY; San Diego.

Generic premiums were used and they are listed below along with the dates they were to have been offered.

Feb 3–Mar 4: Matchbox MiniFlexies (small rubber vehicles)

were offered. Each of the 10 vehicles came in several colors: blue, green, orange, pink, and yellow. The name of the vehicle appeared on the side and the Matchbox and Lesney name were on the bottom. Matchbox is a registered trademark of Lesney Products, London, England. These items were not polybagged and were available in retail stores or directly from the Diener Company.

Mar 4–17: The O'Grimacy inflatable became a hand puppet when the extra bottom piece was cut along the dotted line.

Mar 18–31: A French Fry Flute was originally scheduled to be offered, but was not available on time due to production delays. McDonaldland Miniature Yo-Yos were substituted. These came in red, purple, blue or yellow with a character decal on the $1^3/_8$" x $^3/_4$" body portion. A durable polystyrene ring was attached at the end of the string and slipped over the body of the yo-yo to keep the string from unraveling.

Apr 1–14: The Sundae Smile Saucer originally used in Round Top Test II was once again issued. (see RO7065)

Apr 15–30: McDonaldland Mystery Games were "magic slate" lift up pieces with a red border across the top. Each measured 2" x 4" and was copyrighted 1978. Games included were a maze, tic-tac-toe, connect the dots, and a word guess. Instructions for playing the game were on back of each piece.

May 1–15: The French Fry Ring was an X-O graph – the fries disappeared when the ring moved. It was an adjustable plastic square ring with rounded corners, measuring 1.3" x 1.3"

May 16 - June 3: Ronald piloted the Styro-Glider: punch-out wings and body on a card. Slip the wings through the body to assemble. The glider was $4^3/_8$" and came in red and yellow.

June 4–10: Again the French Fry Flute was scheduled, but production problems still existed. The Spinning Top from Round Test III was used instead (see RO7105).

June 11: The first national Happy Meal began. (see CIRCUS WAGON, 1979).

GE4101 GE4102 GE4103 GE4104

GE4105 GE4107 GE4109 GE4110

Premiums

GE4101	MiniFlexies: Baja Buggy (4101), Beach Hopper (4102), Cosmobile (4103), Datsun 126X (4104), Fandango (4105), Hairy Hustler (4106), Hi Tailer (4107), Mercedes 350SL (4108), Planet Scout (4109), Turbo Fury (4110)	50¢ - 1
GE4111	O'Grimacy Inflatable, uncut	4 - 8
GE4112	Yo-Yo, Big Mac (4112), blue; Grimace (4113), purple; Hamburglar (4114), yellow; Ronald (4115), red Sundae Smile Saucer (See RO7065)	3 - 5
GE4116	Mystery Game: Big Mac Tic-Tac-Toe (4116), Mayor Word Guess (4117), Professor Dot Game (4118), Ronald Maze (4119)	4 - 6

UNCLE O'GRIMACEY

GE4111

GE4120   GE4120   GE4120

GET ONE INSIDE EVERY HAPPY MEAL

MATCHBOX® **MiniFlexies**
OFFER GOOD UNTIL MARCH 25, WHILE SUPPLY LASTS.

GE4142

MATCHBOX® MINIFLEXIES 10 IN ALL. ONE CAR INSIDE EVERY HAPPY MEAL.

"Matchbox"® is a registered trademark of Lesney Products and Company, Limited, London, England

GE4140

GE4113   GE4114   GE4115

Ronald McDonald MAZE   MAYOR McCHEESE's WORD GUESS   THE PROFESSOR'S DOT GAME   BIG MAC TIC TAC TOE

GE4119   GE4117   GE4118   GE4116

GE4130   GE4131   GE4132

GE4133

GE4134

GE4121

GE4120	French Fry Ring, yellow, green, red	6 - 8
GE4121	Ronald Styro–Glider	4 - 8
	Spinning Top (see RO7105`)	

Boxes

GE4130	What and Why/Smart Duck	30 - 50
GE4131	Chef in Teacup/Bird in Measuring Cup	30 - 50
GE4132	Animal Riddles	30 - 50
GE4133	Circus/Lion/Ronald/Captain	30 - 50
GE4134	Skyscrapers/Statue of Liberty	30 - 50

Point of Purchase

GE4140	Translite, MiniFlexies, menu board	15 - 20
GE4141	Counter Card, MiniFlexie, plastic	10 - 13
GE4142	Register Topper, MiniFlexies, red, padded cardboard	10 - 13

GHOSTBUSTERS (See REAL GHOSTBUSTERS)

GIGGLES & GAMES, 1982

This was a national option Happy Meal which ran June 28 – Aug 29, 1982 and in other areas, Aug 24 – Oct 21. Six boxes were designed so each became a game when it was cut and flattened out. Each region selected their own premiums from McDonald's suppliers.

Suggested items from M-B Sales for this promotion included: Tickle Feather Sponge, Tic–Tac–Teeth Slate, Goblin Caller, Ronald Scissors, Hamburglar Sponge, McDonaldland Game Top, Ronald Very Long Whistle, Grimace Very Long Whistle, Hamburglar Comb & Goblin Groomer, Ronald Flying Wheel, Ronald & Grimace Forks and Spoons.

Boxes

GI4500	Bumper Car Tag Game	8 - 12
GI4501	Make–a–Face Chase	8 - 12
GI4502	Monster Marathon Game	8 - 12
GI4503	Outer Space Battle Game	8 - 12
GI4504	Road Rally Game	8 - 12
GI4505	Sunken Treasure Game	8 - 12

Point of Purchase

| GI4510 | Translite, menu board/drive-thru (large) | 10 - 15 |

GI4500   GI4501   GI4502

GI4503   GI4504   GI4505

GO3001   GO3002   GO3003

| GI4511 | Message Center Insert | 10 - 15 |
| GI4512 | Permanent Display Header Card | 6 - 8 |

GLO–TRONS (See SPACESHIP, 1986)

GOING PLACES, 1982

Going Places ran Feb 21 – Apr 28, 1982 and again in 1983. Six boxes were designed, but regions developed their own premiums or purchased generic ones from McDonald's suppliers: K-Promotions, M-B Sales and A/D Enterprises.

Suggested items from M-B Sales for this promotion included:

Jolly Jet Sponge, Going Places Cup, McDonaldland Hockey, Goblins Horseshoes, Goblins Bowling, Ronald Sponge, Grimace Sponge, Hamburglar Sponge, Birdie Sponge, McDonaldland Character Face Magnets, Ronald and Grimace Forks & Spoons, Ronald and Grimace Combs, Ronald Scissors, Ronald Flying Wheel, Grimace Whistle, and Goblin Caller.

Boxes

GO3001	Bi-Plane	4 - 8
GO3002	Dune Buggy	4 - 8
GO3003	Elephant	4 - 8
GO3004	Fire Engine	4 - 8

GI4510

GO3010

GO3004   GO3005   GO3006

GO5301

GO5300

GO5460

GO3005	Paddle-Wheeler	4 - 8
GO3006	Steam Engine	4 - 8
Point of Purchase		
GO3010	Translite, menu board/drive-thru (large)	10 - 15
GO3011	Message Center Insert, cardboard	10 - 15

GOOD FRIENDS, 1987

Another generic box series came out in 1987. These were to be used to fill in when stores ran out of regular boxes. Generic or extra premiums were to be used.

CAUTION: May contain small parts. Not intended for children under 3. Ask about special toys for kids under 3.

GO5305

Boxes

GO5300	Clean Sweep	1 - 4
GO5301	Snapshot Shuffle	1 - 4
Point of Purchase		
GO5305	Translite, menu board	6 - 10
GO5306	Translite, drive-thru	5 - 8

GOOD MORNING, 1991

Premiums themed around kid's morning time activities highlighted this national Happy Meal from Jan 4 thru 31, 1991. During Week #3, a 4-oz box sample of Nestlé's Juicy-Juice was given with the cup in areas where permitted. In ME a 6-oz can was substituted due to local laws. The drinking cup was also used as the "Under 3" offer. The toothbrush, clock and comb each came in a printed polybag.

Premiums

GO5450	Ronald Toothbrush, yellow (Ronald getting out of bed), Week 1	1 - 3
GO5451	Ronald Play Clock, yellow (hands move and glow in the dark), Week 2	1 - 3
GO5452	Ronald Drink Cup, white (2-oz cup of Ronald w/bunny), Week 3	1 - 3
GO5453	Character Comb, 5-pieces which snap together (pc #1: Ronald/red, #2 Fry Kid/ green, #3 Birdie/yellow, #4 Grimace/ purple, #5 Hamburglar/orange	1 - 3
Sack		
GO5460	Good Morning	1 - 2
Point of Purchase		
GO5465	Translite, menu board	6 - 10
GO5466	Translite, drive-thru	4 - 8

GOOD SPORTS, 1984

McDonald Olympic involvement produced the Good Sports Happy Meal, Feb 5 – Apr 15, 1984. McDonaldland characters

GO5452   Juice for GO5452   GO5451

GO5450   GO5453

GO5465

GO5706	Sam the Olympic Eagle/Basketball	3 - 6
Boxes		
GO5715	Skiing	2 - 6
GO5716	Sledding	2 - 6
GO5717	Basketball	2 - 6
GO5718	Gymnastics	2 - 6
Point of Purchase		
GO5725	Translite, menu board/drive-thru	10 - 15
GO5726	Message Center Insert, cardboard	10 - 15
GO5727	Permanent Display Header Card	4 - 6

GO5705   GO5706   GO5703   GO5704   GO5701   GO5702

GRAVEDALE HIGH, 1991

This Mar 8 – Apr 12, 1991 regional promotion was connected with the NBC Saturday morning cartoon series, "Rick Moranis in Gravedale High". This animation of the star featured him as Max Schneider, a teacher assigned to a class of teenage monster misfits at Gravedale High.

Premiums

GR1101	Frankentyke, green face, when hands move tongue comes out, Set 1	3 - 6
GR1102	Sid (the Invisible Kid), purple, hands & feet move, Set 2	3 - 6
GR1103	Vinnie Stoker, orange casket, turn the knob on bottom and lid opens, Set 3	3 - 6
GR1104	Cleofatra, yellow, rocks back & forth, Set 4	3 - 6
GR1105	Same as GR1104, except "Under 3" package	– – 6
Sack, 7" x 13½"		
GR1110	Crossword Puzzle	1 - 3
Point of Purchase		
GR1115	Translite, menu board	6 - 10

GO5715

were featured in sports activities. The 6 puffy stickers had a 1984 copyright on the front except for Sam the Eagle (1981). There were 2 boxes depicting sports in the Winter Olympics and 2 centering on the Summer Olympic Games .

Premiums

GO5701	Birdie/Soccer Ball	3 - 6
GO5702	Grimace/Sled	3 - 6
GO5703	Hamburglar/Hockey	3 - 6
GO5704	Mayor McCheese/Skiing	3 - 6
GO5705	Ronald/Ice Skating	3 - 6

GO5716   GO5717   GO5718

GR1115

GR1110

HA1501   HA1502

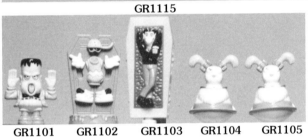

GR1101   GR1102   GR1103   GR1104   GR1105

GR1116   Translite, drive-thru   4 - 8

HALLOWEEN, 1985

Halloween Pails were introduced by McDonald's in the Boston and central New York areas Oct 11–31, 1985. Five pails are known with a 1985 copyright. The pails have 5 names, but only 3 different faces. Only 1 of the pails with the same face on it was used in any one area. Each vacuformed pail came with a handle and a lid which had four $1/2$" openings of 12-hole grid mesh.

Premiums
HA1500	McPunky, orange		8 - 10
HA1501	McPunk'n, orange (same face as HA1500)		8 - 10
HA1502	McGoblin, orange		8 - 10
HA1503	McJack, orange (same face as HA1502)		8 - 10
HA1504	McBoo, orange		8 - 10

HA1500   HA1504   HA1503

Point of Purchase
HA1510   Translite, menu board/drive-thru (large)   15 - 20

HALLOWEEN, 1986

The 3-piece pumpkin pails went national in 1986 (Oct 13 – 30). The lids in 1986 had 6 open $1/2$" holes near the center of the lid. The faces were the same as those used in the 1985 test, but slightly smaller.

Premiums
HA1515	McBoo, orange	1 - 4
HA1516	McGoblin, orange	1 - 4
HA1517	McPunk'n, orange	1 - 4

Point of Purchase
HA1520	Translite, menu board/drive-thru (large)	6 - 12
HS1521	Message Center Insert, cardboard	6 - 12

HALLOWEEN, 1987

The Oct 16–31, 1987 promotion used the same buckets as were used in 1986, but the vent holes in the lids were changed so kids' fingers could not get caught in them. Small cross pieces were added to the holes so they were no longer entirely open.

HA1510

70

Premiums

HA1525	McBoo, orange	1 - 2
HA1526	McGoblin, orange	1 - 2
HA1527	McPunk'n, orange	1 - 2

Point of Purchase

HA1530	Translite, menu board	6 - 10
HA1531	Translite, drive-thru	4 - 8

HALLOWEEN, 1988 (See ZOO–FACE, 1988)

HALLOWEEN, 1989

For this year's Oct 6–31 campaign, two new designs on the 3-piece Jack-o-Lantern pails appeared for the national promotion. The green and white pails did not have names printed on the back as was done in past years. For the third pail, stores received a combination of the 3 designs used in 1987.

Premiums

HA1541	White Pail (ghost face)	1 - 3
HA1542	Green Pail (witch face & hat)	1 - 3
	Orange Pail (see HA1525-27)	

Point of Purchase

HA1545	Translite, menu board	6 - 10
HA1546	Translite, drive-thru	4 - 8

HA1545

HALLOWEEN, 1990

More changes to the Halloween pails occurred in 1990. Three new faces and three new colors added interest to this promotion which ran Oct 5–25. No names appeared on the back of the 3-piece (pail, lid and handle) buckets.

Premiums

HA1555	Day Glo Pumpkin, neon orange	1 - 2
HA1556	Glow-in-the-Dark Ghost, white	1 - 2
HA1557	Day Glo Witch, neon green (witch hat lid)	1 - 2

Point of Purchase

HA1565	Translite, menu board	6 - 10
HA1566	Translite, drive-thru	4 - 8

HALLOWEEN, 1991 (see McBOO BAGS, 1991)

HAPPY HOLIDAYS, 1984

This Christmas promotion featured Mrs. Grossman's Paper

HA1565

Co. cards and stickers designed exclusively for McDonald's. The national option program ran Nov 23 – Dec 24, 1984.

Premiums

HA5000	Gingerbread Holiday House Card/Sticker Sheet	4 - 12
HA5001	Toy Train Set Card/Sticker Sheet	4 - 12

Boxes

HA5005	Ronald/Sleigh, red box	2 - 5
HA5006	Gingerbread/Forest, green box	2 - 5

Point of Purchase

HA5010	Translite, menu board/drive-thru (large)	10 - 15
HA5011	Message Center Insert, cardboard	5 - 15
HA5012	Permanent Display Header Card	4 - 6
HA5013	Menu Board Premium Lug-On	4 - 6

HAPPY PAIL, 1983

Three sail pails were provided as premiums in this Upper New York State regional "McDonald's Happy Pail" promotion.

HA5010

HA5006   HA5005

HA5655

HA5650   HA5651   HA5652

HA5672   HA5673

HA5670   HA5671

Each premium came in 4 parts: pail, lid (with 4 holes in it), handle and shovel. The lid and handle matched the color of the bucket. Printed on each pail was "Pail and shovel safety tested for children 3 years and over." The bottom of the pail was imprinted with "Genpak Corporation, Glens Falls, NY, mammoth containers." The pails featured the McDonaldland characters and carried a 1983 McDonald Corporation copyright date.

Premiums

HA5650	Ronald & Mayor under Beach Umbrella, pink pail/pink shovel	8 - 15
HA5651	Ronald in an Inner Tube, white pail/purple shovel	8 - 15
HA5652	Airplane Pulling Banner, yellow pail/yellow shovel	8 - 15

Point of Purchase

HA5655	Translite, menu board/drive-thru (large)	10 - 15

HAPPY PAIL, 1984 (Olympic)

An Olympic theme tie-in with a Happy Pail regional promotion ran May 18 – June 17, 1984. The 4 pails had matching colored lids and handles and each came with a yellow shovel. "Safety tested for children 3 years and over" was molded on the shovel. The lids had 4 open vent holes near the outside rim.

Premiums

HA5670	Athletics, beige	1 - 4
HA5671	Cycling, yellow	1 - 4
HA5672	Olympic Games, white	1 - 4
HA5673	Swimming, blue	1 - 4

Point of Purchase

HA5680	Translite, menu board/drive-thru (large)	8 - 12
HA5681	Message Center Insert, cardboard	8 - 12
HA5682	Counter Display, 1 bucket per week	50 - 70

HAPPY PAIL, 1986

Happy Pails were back in 1986 (May 30 – July 6) with new designs showing McDonald's characters at play. A contribution

HA5682

was made to the Ronald McDonald Children's Charities and Ronald McDonald House for each pail meal sold. There was also a counter collection display where other donations could be made. The 5 pails were white with color graphics. The handle and special designed "sand sifter" lid were color matched. Either a red rake or yellow shovel came with each pail.

Premiums

HA5690	Beach, blue handle & lid	1 - 3
HA5691	Parade, orange handle & lid	1 - 3
HA5692	Picnic, yellow handle & lid	1 - 3
HA5693	Treasure Hunt, red handle & lid	1 - 3
HA5694	Vacation, green handle & lid	1 - 3

HA5699

HA5680

HA5691   HA5692

HA5694

HA5693   HA5690

HAPPY TEETH

A "Reach" youth-size toothbrush was offered in a Happy Meal tie-in with Dental Health Month. The number of premiums, colors, box, and location have not been determined. The 1983 copyrighted translite showed a smiley tooth with a Happy Meal box and toothbrush and was titled "Happy Teeth!"

Premiums

HA5720	Reach Toothbrush	?

Point of Purchase

HA5730	Translite, menu board	15 - 20

HATS, 1990

This regional campaign ran in selected southern states from Sept 7 to Oct 4, 1990. Each hat came with a character decal on front. Four different clear plastic bottoms with embossed McDonald's characters snapped on the hat to close the container. Each of these pieces were formed to fit each hat shape.

HA5696

Point of Purchase

HA5696	Translite, menu board	6 - 10
HA5697	Translite, drive-thru	4 - 8
HA5698	Display (collection for Children's Charity)	20 - 40
HA5699	Counter Mat	2 - 7
HA5700	Ceiling Dangler w/premiums	10 - 20

Premiums

HA8000	Birdie Derby Hat, green, Fry Girl/Ronald	4 - 10
HA8001	Fry Guy Safari Hat, orange, Fry Guy/Fry Girl	4 - 10
HA8002	Grimace Construction Hat, yellow, Hamburglar/Professor	4 - 10
HA8003	Ronald Fireman's Hat, red, Fry Guy/Birdie	4 - 10

HA8000   HA8001   HA8003   HA8002

HA5730

HI4510

HO4510

HO4511

HO4512

HI4501   HI4502

Point of Purchase

HA8010	Translite, menu board	8 - 12
HA8011	Translite, drive-thru	6 - 10

HIGH FLYING KITE, 1986

Wing-shaped kites were the premiums for a 1987 Happy Meal in the North Eastern states. Each Happy Meal included string and a handle to be used when flying the 24" x 15½" kite. Due the length of the kites, they were issued in a bag.

Premiums

HI4500	Birdie	5 - 20
HI4501	Hamburglar	5 - 20
HI4502	Ronald	5 - 20
Box		
HI4510	Kites Flying	10 - 15
Point of Purchase		
HI4515	Translite, menu board	10 - 15
HI4516	Translite, drive-thru	8 - 12

HOOK, 1991

A national Happy Meal (Dec 6, 1991 – Jan 2, 1992) featured tub toy premiums as a tie-in with the Steven Spielberg movie, *Hook*. The 4 premiums were packaged in printed bags.

Premiums

HO4500	Peter Pan, floats & rolls, 3 pcs	1 - 3
HO4501	Mermaid, winds up, then swims	1 - 3
HO4502	Captain Hook, sails the waves, 2 pcs	1 - 3
HO4503	Rufio, squirts	1 - 3
Boxes		
HO4510	Jolly Roger	1 - 3
HO4511	Nevertree	1 - 3
HO4512	Pirate Town	1 - 3
HO4513	Wendy's London House	1 - 3
Point of Purchase		
HO4520	Translite, menu board	8 - 10
HO4521	Translite, drive-thru	6 - 8
HO4522	Counter Display w/premiums	50 - 75

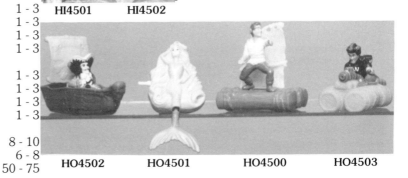

HO4502   HO4501   HO4500   HO4503

74

HO4513

HO7020

HO4522

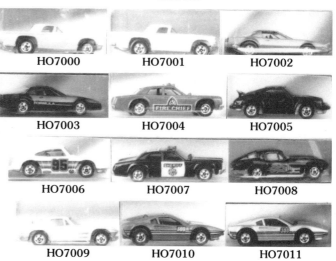

HO7000	HO7001	HO7002
HO7003	HO7004	HO7005
HO7006	HO7007	HO7008
HO7009	HO7010	HO7011

HO7027

HOT WHEELS, 1988

The first time Hot Wheels were featured as a Happy Meal premium occurred in selected regions during 1988. Each car came in a blister pack with a card identical to those sold in retail stores. For this promotion a single box listing all 12 cars on the back of the box was used. In 1983, McDonald's <u>sold</u> Hot Wheels cars as a self-liquidator, but there was no connection to the Happy Meal program at that time.

Premiums

HO7000	'57 T-Bird, turquoise	2 - 5
HO7001	'57 T-Bird, white	2 - 5
HO7002	'80s Firebird, blue	2 - 5
HO7003	'80s Firebird, black	2 - 5
HO7004	Fire Chief, red	2 - 5
HO7005	P-911 Turbo, black	2 - 5
HO7006	P-911 Turbo, white	2 - 5
HO7007	Sheriff Patrol, black	2 - 5
HO7008	Split Window '63, black	2 - 5
HO7009	Split Window '63, silver	2 - 5
HO7010	Street Beast, red	2 - 5
HO7011	Street Beast, silver	2 - 5

Box

HO7020	Speed Ramp	2 - 5

Point of Purchase

HO7025	Translite, menu board	10 - 15
HO7026	Translite, drive-thru	8 - 12

HO7027   Counter Display w/premiums   100 - 150

HOT WHEELS/BARBIE (See BARBIE/HOT WHEELS)

I LIKE BIKES, 1990

Rockford, IL and South Carolina ran the "I Like Bikes Happy Meal" in July 1990. Each of the bike premiums came in a polybag except for the basket (with attachment straps in a polybag) and lid. Two sacks were designed for this promotion.

Premiums

IL3000	Birdie Spinner, red airplane w/yellow propeller, attachment clamp & screws	10 - 15

IL3001	Fry Guy's Horn, blue horn, attachment clamp & screws	10 - 15
IL3002	Grimace's Rear View Reflector, purple mirror, attachment clamp & screws	10 - 15
IL3003	Ronald Bike Basket, yellow, lid & 2 attachment straps	15 - 20

Sacks, 8¹/₂" x 12"

| IL3010 | Ronald on Bike | 2 - 4 |
| IL3011 | Ronald, Hamburglar, Grimace on Bikes | 2 - 4 |

Point of Purchase

IL3015	Translite, menu board	10 - 15
IL3016	Translite, drive-thru	8 - 12
IL3017	Counter Display w/premiums	100 - 150

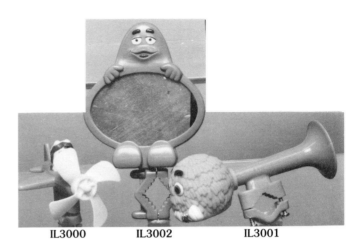

IL3000   IL3002   IL3001

JUNGLE BOOK, 1990

The July 6 – Aug 2, 1990 Happy Meal was based on the re-release of Walt Disney Studio's film, *The Jungle Book*. The animal premiums were the first motorized action figures

IL3010   IL3011

IL3015

IL3003

McDonald's ever did. The "Under 3" premiums were of 1 piece and had no moveable parts. **NOTE:** Some areas moved the starting date to July 20 so the introduction of the $1.99 Happy Meal could be incorporated into the schedule. (see SUMMER SURPRISE, 1990)

Premiums

| JU8500 | Baloo, the bear, gray, #1 | 1 - 3 |

IL3017   JU8522

	JU8510	JU8511	JU8512	JU8513

JU8500	JU8501	JU8502	JU8503	JU8505	JU8504

JU8501	King Louie, the orangutan, orange, #2	1 - 3
JU8502	Kaa, the snake, green, #3	1 - 3
JU8503	Shere Khan, the tiger, orange, #4	1 - 3
JU8504	Junior, the elephant, gray (Under 3)	2 - 6
JU8505	Mowgli, boy in clayware pot, green (Under 3)	2 - 6

Boxes

JU8510	Baloo	1 - 3
JU8511	Hidden Animal	1 - 3
JU8512	Kaa	1 - 3
JU8513	King Louie	1 - 3

Point of Purchase

JU8520	Translite, menu board, plastic, X-O graphic	10 - 20
JU8521	Translite, drive-thru	6 - 10
JU8522	Counter Display w/premiums	75 - 125
JU8523	Dangler, 1 for each premium, each	3 - 5
JU8524	Crew Button	1 - 2

KISSYFUR, 1987

Several markets participated in the regional Kissyfur Happy Meal from Apr 24 – June 4, 1987. Some of these areas were: St. Louis; Memphis; Huntsville, AL; Booneville, MS; Corinth, MS; Chattanooga and San Antonio. This Saturday morning cartoon series on NBC featured Kissyfur (a bear) and his father as they leave a circus and end up living in a swamp. Half of the 8 figures had a flocked finish. All were copyrighted 1981 by Phil Mendez. The packages carried a safety warning with a "made in China" notation.

Premiums

KI5001	Beehonie – rabbit, white, flocked	2 - 8
KI5002	Duane – pig, pink, flocked	2 - 8
KI5003	Floyd – alligator, green, smooth	2 - 5
KI 5004	Gus – Kissyfur's father, brown/yellow, smooth	2 - 5
KI5005	Jolene – alligator, green, smooth	2 - 5
KI5006	Kissyfur – small bear, brown, smooth	2 - 5
KI5007	Lennie – wart hog, brown, flocked	2 - 8
KI5008	Toot – beaver, gray, flocked	2 - 8

Box

KI5015	Gus Juggling Apples	2 - 5

KI5001	KI5002	KI5003	KI5004	KI5005	KI5007	KI5006	KI5008

JU8521

KI5020

KI5015 LE2010 LE2011

LE2035 LE2036 LE2037 LE2038

Point of Purchase

KI5020	Translite, menu board	10 - 15
KI5021	Translite, drive-thru	8 - 12

LEGO BUILDING SETS, 1983, Test

Lego Building Sets were tested in Salt Lake City in June of 1983. A bounce-back offer was included in each pouch – purchase 3 Happy Meals, make a $10 retail Lego purchase and send in to redemption center for a free Lego set worth $6.50. Four Duplo Sets (larger blocks with rounded edges) were made available upon request for the "Under 3" premiums.

Premiums

LE2001	Truck model, red border pouch, Week 1	– – 20
LE2002	Ship model, blue border pouch, Week 2	– – 20
LE2003	Helicopter model, yellow border pouch, Week 3	– – 20
LE2004	Airplane model, green border pouch, Week 4	– – 20
LE2005	Duplo Set, Week 1 (Under 3)	– – 20
LE2006	Duplo Set, Week 2 (Under 3)	– – 20
LE2007	Duplo Set, Week 3 (Under 3)	– – 20
LE2008	Duplo Set, Week 4 (Under 3)	– – 20

Box

LE2010	Master the Maze, '83 copyright	15 - 20
LE2011	What's Wrong?, '83 copyright	15 - 20

Point of Purchase

LE2015	Translite, menu board/drive-thru (large)	15 - 20

LEGO BUILDING SETS, 1984

Lego Building Sets went national with the Oct 26 – Nov 25, 1984 promotion. The Lego Company was founded in 1932 by Ole Kirk Christiansen in Denmark. The plastic Lego bricks were first produced in 1949. The present Lego plastic coupling system was introduced in 1958. With Legos, just 6 bricks can

be combined 102,981,500 different ways. There was a bounce-back coupon in each package similar to the one used in the test market. Two Duplo Building Sets were packaged with the statement "Ages 1–4".

Premiums

LE2025	Truck, red, 17 pcs, red pkg, Set 1	– – 8
LE2026	Ship, 4 colors, 27 pcs, blue pkg, Set 2	– – 8
LE2027	Helicopter, yellow, 19 pcs, yellow pkg, Set 3	– – 8

LE2040

LE2025	LE2026	LE2027	LE2028

LE2029	LE2030	LE2205	LE2204

LE2210	LE2211	LE2212	LE2213

LE2220

LE2223

LE2515   LE2516

LE2522

LE2517   LE2518

LE2028   Airplane, 4 colors, 18 pcs, green pkg, Set 4   – - 8
LE2029   Boat/Sailor, blue, 5 pcs, blue pkg (ages 1-4)   – - 10
LE2030   Bird/Eye, red, 5 pcs, red pkg (ages 1-4)   – - 10

Boxes
LE2035   Find the Fry Guys, '84 copyright   2 - 5
LE2036   Master the Maze, '84 copyright   2 - 5
LE2037   Ship Shapes, '84 copyright   2 - 5
LE2038   What's Wrong?, '84 copyright   2 - 5

Point of Purchase
LE2040   Translite, menu board/drive-thru (large)   10 - 15

LE2041   Message Center Insert, cardboard   10 - 15
LE2042   Counter Display w/premiums &   150 - 200
          Ronald constructed from Legos
LE2043   Dangler, 1 for each premium, each   6 - 8
LE2044   Tray Liner   2 - 4

LEGO BUILDING SETS (Little Travelers), 1985

A Little Travelers Lego Building Set Happy Meal was run in Oklahoma in 1985. All premiums were the same as those used in 1984; the boxes were designed with the "Little Travelers" notation. Super Travelers (ST) Building Sets for older kids were

LE2520   LE2521

80

LE2522

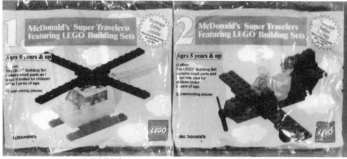

LE2504   LE2505

LE2506   LE2507

sold for 59¢ as a tie-in promotion. These sets were <u>not</u> given in the Happy Meal, but were a self-liquidator for ages 5 years and up. The promotion for both sets was entitled "Lego Toy Days". The circular counter display featured Little Travelers on one half; Super Travelers on the other.

Premiums
Same as those used in 1984 (see LE2025-30)
Self-Liquidators (Super Travelers)
LE2504	Helicopter, yellow, 36 pcs, #1	– - 20
LE2505	Airplane and Pilot, blue, 26 pcs, #2	– - 20
LE2506	Cruise Boat, 38 pcs, #3	– - 20
LE2507	Race Car and Driver, 19 pcs, #4	– - 20

Boxes (Little Travelers)
LE2515	Captain/Tug Boat	2 - 8
LE2516	Grimace/Vacation	2 - 8
LE2517	Grimace/Golden Gate Bridge	2 - 8
LE2518	Ronald/Globe	2 - 8

Point of Purchase
LE2520	Translite, Little Travelers	15 - 20
LE2521	Translite, Super Travelers	15 - 20
LE2522	Translite, Lego Toy Days	15 - 20
LE2523	Counter Display (LT/ST)	75 - 125

LEGO BUILDING SETS, 1986
Another national Lego Happy Meal ran Oct 31 – Nov 26, 1986. There was a special offer inside the package telling how to obtain another Lego Set. For this promotion the underaged premiums carried a notation for "Ages 1½ - 4".

Premiums
LE2200	Race Car, 16 pcs, red border pkg, Set A	– - 5
LE2201	Tanker Boat, 27 pcs, blue border pkg, Set B	– - 5
LE2202	Helicopter, 18 pcs, yellow border pkg, Set C	– - 5
LE2203	Airplane, 18 pcs, green border pkg, Set D	– - 5
LE2204	Bird w/Eye, 5 pcs, broken red border pkg (ages 1½-4)	– - 6
LE2205	Boat w/Sailor, 5 pcs, broken blue border pkg (ages 1½-4)	– - 6

Boxes
LE2210	Captain/Tug Boat	1 - 4
LE2211	Grimace/Vacation	1 - 4
LE2212	Grimace/Golden Gate Bridge	1 - 4
LE2213	Ronald/Globe	1 - 4

Point of Purchase
LE2220	Translite, menu board	6 - 10

LE2221	Translite, drive-thru	4 - 8
LE2222	Message Center Insert, cardboard	6 - 10
LE2223	Counter Display w/premiums	50 - 80

LEGO MOTION, 1989
Lego Systems of Denmark and McDonald's teamed up for a third national Lego Building Set Happy Meal which ran July 28 – Aug 24, 1989. The number of premiums was increased and another special offer redeemable for the customer's choice of 1 of 4 Lego sets was included in each package. The 8 Lego brick sets each had special pieces which provided motion; i.e., wheels, propellers, etc. Brochures in the package gave instructions on how to combine different sets to make super-size models. As in previous Lego promotions, Duplo Block Sets were

McDonald's Happy Meal presents
LEGO MOTION
COLLECT ALL 8 BUILDING SETS WHILE SUPPLIES LAST.

LE2727

LE2715   LE2717   LE2718   LE2716

LE2728
(Shows LE2700-07)

LE3410

LE2708   LE2709

available for "Ages 1½ – 4". These packages had a broken black border on them. The 4 boxes were designed so that 2 or more of them could be lined up to form a land, water or sky scene – instructions were printed on the bottom of the box.

Premiums

LE2700	Gyro Bird Helicopter, 19 pcs, 1a	– -	4
LE2701	Turbo Force Vehicle, 10 pcs, 1b	– -	4
LE2702	Swamp Stinger Boat, 16 pcs, 2a	– -	4
LE2703	Lightning Striker Plane, 14 pcs, 2b	– -	4
LE2704	Land Laser Car, 13 pcs, 3a	– -	4
LE2705	Sea Eagle Seaplane, 15 pcs, 3b	– -	4
LE2706	Wind Whirler Helicopter, 17 pcs, 4a	– -	4
LE2707	Sea Skimmer Boat, 17 pcs, 4b	– -	4
LE2708	Giddy the Gater, 6 pcs (Under 4)	– -	5
LE2709	Tuttle the Turtle, 6 pcs (Under 4)	– -	5

Boxes

LE2715	Lake	1 -	3
LE2716	Traffic Copter/Clocks	1 -	3
LE2717	Road Race	1 -	3
LE2718	Ronald in Helicopter	1 -	3

Point of Purchase

LE2725	Translite, menu board, motion wheel	10 -	15
LE2726	Translite, drive-thru	4 -	8
LE2727	Counter Display w/premiums	60 -	90
LE2728	Menu Board Premium Lug-On	6 -	8

LE2725

LITTLE ENGINEER, 1987

Kids love trains and 5 train engines were offered with the Little Engineer Happy Meal regional promotion, Feb 9 – Mar 19, 1987. The train engines had moving wheels and were designed to connect together. Each came on a plastic tree and the pieces needed to be snapped together. The "Under 3" premiums were of 1-piece construction with no moving parts. In one corner of each of the 4 boxes used in this promotion was printed the message "Look inside box for decorative stickers", as a sticker sheet was pre-inserted and glued inside each box before they were shipped to the stores.

LI3411   LI3412   LI3413

LI3400   LI3401   LI3402   LI3403   LI3404

LI3406   LI3405

LI3485   LI3488

Premiums

LI3400	Birdie "Sunshine Special", yellow, 3 pcs	2 - 6
LI3401	Fry Girl "Express", blue, 3 pcs	2 - 6
LI3402	Fry Guy "Flyer", bright orange, 3 pcs	2 - 6
LI3403	Grimace "Purple Streak", purple, 3 pcs	2 - 6
LI3404	Ronald "Ronald's Railway", red, 4 pcs	2 - 6
LI3405	Fry Guy Happy Car (Under 3)	1 - 5
LI3406	Grimace Happy Taxi (Under 3)	1 - 5

Boxes

LI3410	Round House	2 - 4
LI3411	Station	2 - 4
LI3412	Trestle/Fry Girls	2 - 4
LI3413	Tunnel	2 - 4

Point of Purchase

LI3418	Translite, menu board/drive-thru (large)	6 - 10
LI3419	Translite, drive-thru (small)	4 - 8
LI3420	Translite, drive-thru strip insert	4 - 8

Premiums

LI3475	Birdie Shovel w/Marigold seeds, orange, #1	1 - 3
LI3476	Fry Kids Planter, turquoise w/ lid & handle, purple, #2	1 - 3
LI3477	Grimace Rake w/radish seeds, green, #3	1 - 3
LI3478	Ronald Water Can, red w/yellow handle, #4	1 - 3
LI3479	Same as LI3475, except it came bagged w/o the seed packet (Under 3)	– - 6

Sacks

LI3485	Birdie's Bouquet	1 - 3
LI3486	Garden Goodies	1 - 3
LI3487	Radish Contest	1 - 3
LI3488	Whose Hose?	1 - 3

Point of Purchase

LI3495	Translite, menu board	6 - 10
LI3496	Translite, drive-thru	4 - 8

LITTLE GARDENER, 1989

McDonald's got ready for spring with the Little Gardener national promotion, Apr 21 – May 18, 1989. The 4 gardening items came polybagged, except for the planter. Burpee seed packets were included with 2 of the tools. Four 8^1/$_2$" x 12", 3-color sacks were used.

LITTLE GOLDEN BOOK, 1982

Little Golden Books, children's storybooks published by Western Publishing, were featured in a Happy Meal which ran July 16 – Aug 23, 1982. The 5 Golden Books offered were like ones sold retail except the inside cover had an imprint which read "This Little Golden Book from McDonald's belongs to" with a line to write in the child's name. Another difference

LI3475-79

LI3495

LI3562

was a coupon page (yellow) at the back which indicated the coupon was to be redeemed at retail outlets, not at McDonald's. Since the books would not fit in the standard size Happy Meal box, a special box was designed. A slot was cut in the front of the box so when the box was opened and the handle folded correctly, the book would fit into the slot. An extra piece of cardboard came with each book to go along side of it so the food would not touch the book.

Premiums

LI3550	*Benji, Fastest Dog in the West*	2 - 5
LI3551	*Country Mouse and the City Mouse*	2 - 5
LI3552	*Monster at the end of this book*	2 - 5
LI3553	*Poky Little Puppy*	2 - 5
LI3554	*Tom and Jerry's Party*	2 - 5

Boxes

LI3558	Little Golden Book	2 - 6

A book in every box
COLLECT ALL 5 BOOKS!

LI3560

Point of Purchase

LI3560	Translite, menu board/drive-thru (large)	10 - 15
LI3561	Message Center Insert, cardboard	10 - 15
LI3562	Counter Card	10 - 15

LI3550

LI3551

LI3552

LI3553

LI3554

LI3566   LI3567

LI3916

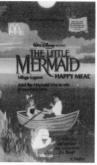

LI3917

LI3558

LI3563	Crew Badge, *Benji*, stick-on, paper	5 - 8
LI3564	Crew Badge, *Country Mouse*, stick-on, paper	5 - 8
LI3565	Crew Badge, *Monster*, stick-on, paper	5 - 8
LI3566	Crew Badge, *Poky*, stick-on, paper	5 - 8
LI3567	Crew Badge, *Tom and Jerry*, stick-on, paper	5 - 8

LITTLE MERMAID, 1989

McDonald's holiday promotion tied-in with the release of Disney's animated film based on a Hans Christian Anderson fairy tale, *The Little Mermaid*. The national Happy Meal dates were Nov 24 – Dec 21, 1989. The 4 tub/bath toys each came in printed polybags. Four boxes were used nationally and 2 4-color sacks were test marketed in the South Bend, IN area.

Premiums

LI3900	Flounder (Ariel's companion fish), squirt toy, yellow, #1	2 - 5
LI3901	Ursula (sea witch octopus), suction cup toy, black, #2	2 - 5
LI3902	Prince Eric (Ariel's hero) & *Sebastian* (the singing crab) boat, yellow, 2-pcs, #3	2 - 5
LI3903	Ariel (The Little Mermaid), floating plastic figure, green tail, orange hair, #4	2 - 5

LI3900   LI3901   LI3902   LI3903

Boxes

LI3910	Ariel's Grotto	1 - 4
LI3911	Sea Garden	1 - 4
LI3912	Ursula's Domain	1 - 4
LI3913	Village Lagoon	1 - 4

Sacks – 7" x 11¼", full color

| LI3916 | Ursula's Domain | 15 - 20 |
| LI3917 | Village Lagoon | 15 - 20 |

Point of Purchase

| LI3920 | Translite, menu board | 10 - 15 |
| LI3921 | Translite, drive-thru | 8 - 10 |

LITTLE TRAVELERS (See LEGO BUILDING SETS (Little Travelers), 1985)

LI3920

LI3910   LI3911   LI3912   LI3913

LO5600

LO5601

LO5610

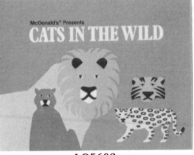

LO5602

LO5603

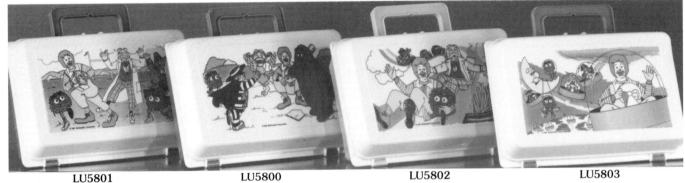

LU5801   LU5800   LU5802   LU5803

LOOK–LOOK BOOKS, 1980

Look-Look Books published by Western Publishing Co. were used as a Happy Meal promotion premium in the St. Louis region in 1980. The counter card read, "Offer good until April 20." The containers are unknown. The four 12-page "Animals of the World" books measured 5¹/₄" x 4" and were polybagged with the McDonald's logo on the back of each book.

Premiums

LO5600	*Animals of the Sea*	5 - 15
LO5601	*Animals That Fly*	5 - 15
LO5602	*Cats in the Wild*	5 - 15
LO5603	*The Biggest Animals*	5 - 15

Point of Purchase

LO5610	Counter Card	10 - 20

LUNCH BOX (unconfirmed)

Four plastic lunch boxes have surfaced which have the McDonald's logo molded on one side with "Whirley Industries, Inc., Warren, PA U.S.A., Patent Pending" molded in the right corner on the other side. These boxes measured 2¹/₂" x 6" x 7¹/₂". This is unconfirmed as a Happy Meal container.

Premiums

LU5200	Light green	5 - 10
LU5201	Yellow	5 - 10
LU5202	Red	5 - 10
LU5203	Blue	5 - 10

LUNCH BOX, 1987 (unconfirmed)

In 1987, 4 different lunch boxes appeared. One-half of the box was white with a colored McDonald character scene; the other half and handle, another color. These carried a 1987 copyright. The time and location of the promotion is unknown.

Premiums

LU5800	Grimace at Bat, white/purple	5 - 10
LU5801	Ronald/Football, white/blue	5 - 10
LU5802	Ronald/Rainbow, white/yellow	5 - 10
LU5803	Ronald/Spaceship, white/red	5 - 10

LUNCH BOX (TV Lunch Bunch), 1987

Another set of 4 lunch boxes were used as premiums/containers for a Happy Meal. This set has been found in Eastern NY. One side of the box resembled a TV set with the picture tube outline and control knobs molded into the plastic. Safety information is also molded on this side. Molded onto the other side was a "Back to School" scene. The handle was *M* shaped. Each box came with a sticker sheet which carried a 1986 copyright. On the back of each sheet were "Safety Tips for Back to School".

Premiums

LU5810	Blue	5 - 10
LU5811	Green	5 - 10
LU5812	Red	5 - 10
LU5813	Yellow	5 - 10
LU5814	Lunch box w/o stickers	5 - 7
LU5815	Lunch Box & separate sticker sheet	10 - 15
LU5816	Sticker sheet only	3 - 5

Point of Purchase

LU5820	Translite, '87 copyright	10 - 20

LU5810

MA0801 MA0800

MA0802 MA0803

MA0804 MA0805 MA0806 MA0807 MA0808

MA0815

MA0816

MAC TONIGHT, 1988/90

The Mac Tonight character became the focus of a regional Happy Meal in California in 1988 and other areas in 1989–1990. Mac Tonight had been featured in other McDonald's promotions singing a take-off of the popular song, *Mack the Knife*. Each of the 6 travel toys contained a non-removeable figure of Mac Tonight. Sets #3 and #6 were slightly different in the 1990 version. All premiums came in a polybag with an insert card. One box was used for the first promotion; a sack, for the later promotion dates.

Premiums

MA0800	Jeep, green, Set 1	2 - 4
MA0801	Sports Car, red Porsche, Set 2	2 - 4
MA0802	Surf Ski/no wheels, yellow, Set 3	3 - 5
MA0803	Surf Ski/3 wheels, yellow, 1990 Set 3	2 - 4
MA0804	Scooter, black, Set 4	2 - 4
MA0805	Motorcycle, red, Set 5	2 - 4
MA0806	Airplane, blue-green, blue lens in Mac's sunglasses, Set 6	3 - 5
MA0807	Airplane, blue-green, black lens in Mac's sunglasses, 1990 Set 6	2 - 4
MA0808	Mac/Skateboard, 1-pc (Under 3)	2 - 4

Box/Sack

MA0815	On the Road, box	1 - 3
MA0816	Mac/Vehicles, sack, white, 7" x 13½"	1 - 3

Point of Purchase

MA0825	Translite, menu board	6 - 10
MA0826	Translite, drive-thru	4 - 8
MA0827	Counter Display w/premiums (not used in 1990 promotion)	75 - 100

MAGIC SHOW, 1985/86

Ronald performs magic tricks in TV commercials and personal appearances. This talent was featured in a national Magic Show Happy Meal from Sept 3 to Oct 20, 1985 in most areas and later during Jan/Feb 1986 in parts of TN, NE, and MO. Each premium ran for 12 days, making this a 7-week promotion. There were really only 4 magic tricks offered, but the use of different colors and characters on these 4 make a total of 7 separate premiums available. The "Under 3" premiums were tub toys.

MA0825

MA0827

MA3510   MA3511   MA3512

Premiums

MA3500 Disappearing Hamburger Patch, 3 pcs on   3 - 5
      a plastic tree, came in 2 colors (red or blue)
      (TRICK: lift off top piece, Hamburger
      appears; lift off top 2 pcs, hamburger vanishes)

MA3501 Magic String Pull, Birdie embossed on case,   3 - 6
      came in 2 colors in a clear polybag (green
      or orange) (TRICK: pull string through
      case, string changes color)

MA3502 Magic Tablet, Ronald holding tablet, blue   3 - 6
      came in clear polybag (TRICK: write
      message on table, pull paper bar across
      and writing disappears)

MA3503 Magic Picture, Grimace or Ronald face   3 - 6
      came in clear polybag (TRICK: pull picture
      panel out and faces changes from black
      and white to color)
      Grimace Tub Toy (see SH5054)
      Fry Guy & Friend Tub Toy (see SH5055)

Boxes

MA3510 Ghost Writer   2 - 5
MA3511 Eggs with Legs   2 - 5
MA3512 Sticky Card Trick   2 - 5
MA3513 Tug o' War   2 - 5

Point of Purchase

MA3520 Translite, menu board/drive-thru (large)   8 - 12
MA3521 Translite, drive-thru (small)   6 - 8
MA3522 Message Center Insert, cardboard   8 - 12
MA3523 Permanent Display Header Card   4 - 6

MA3500

MA3501

MA3513

MA3503 (Ronald)   MA3503 (Grimace)   MA3502

MA3524 Menu Board Premium Lug-On   4 - 6

MATCHBOX SUPER GT, 1988

Sixteen Matchbox Super GT cars were the premiums for an OK regional Happy Meal. The date on the box is 1987, so the promotion probably ran in late 1987 or 1988. Each car came in a clear polybag with a small slip of paper bearing the "Safety tested for children 3 and over. Caution: May contain small parts. Not intended for children under 3. Made in China. Printed in Hong Kong" message. On the bottom of each car was the Matchbox name, "Made in China, Super GT, 1985" and a model number. This number is listed at the end of each car description below. Four numbers (BR 7/8, BR 9/10, BR 21/22, BR 27/28) appeared twice as these models were used two times, but in different colors. These cars were also sold in retail stores. One box was provided with a built-in speed ramp.

Premiums

MA7501 Almond car, #16, black stripes (BR 27/28)   – – 10
MA7502 Beige car, Starfire, red stripes (BR 23/24)   – – 10
MA7503 Blue car, #8, red flame graphics (BR 37/38)   – – 10
MA7504 Metallic blue car, yellow–green graphics   – – 10
      (BR 9/10)
MA7505 Green car, #8, white & yellow graphics   – – 10
      (BR 27/28)
MA7506 Orange car, #6, blue & white stripes   – – 10
      (BR 21/22)

MA3520

MA7501	MA7502	MA7503	MA7507
MA7506	MA7515	MA7516	MA7508
MA7511	MA7505	MA7510	MA7514
MA7513	MA7504	MA7509	MA7512

MA7507 Orange car, Turbo, white flame graphics (BR 7/8) – – 10

MA7508 Silver gray car, #3 Drive (BR 35/36) – – 10

MA7509 Silver gray car, green & red stripes (BR 5/6) – – 10

MA7510 Silver gray car, Super GT, black & blue – – 10

MA7530

MA7532

stripes (BR 21/22)

MA7511 White car, #1, red flame graphics (BR 9/10) – – 10

MA7512 White car, #18, red stripe (BR 19/20) – – 10

MA7513 White car, #45, Racer, red stripes (BR 33/34) – – 10

MA7514 White car, yellow & blue graphics (BR 7/8) – – 10

MA7515 Yellow car, #19, red & blue stripes) (BR 31/32) – – 10

MA7516 Mustard yellow car, dark blue & orange stripes (BR 29/30) – – 10

Box

MA7525 Super GT/8 cars 4 - 6

Point of Purchase

MA7530 Translite, menu board 10 - 15

MA7531 Translite, drive-thru 8 - 12

MA7532 Counter Card w/premiums 100 - 150

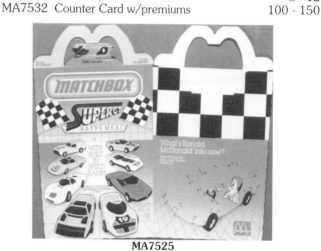

MA7525

McBOO BAGS, 1991

In 1991, the McBoo Bags were the primary Halloween premiums. As a safety factor, all 3 bags glowed in the dark. However, the three 1990 Halloween pails were also used to meet the demand in some areas. A safety sticker was added to the pails and the handle design was changed to reflect that used on the Bunny Pails (a stylized McDonald's *M* which formed "bunny ears"). The safety sticker read: "Made in the United States of America. Caution: Not to be used as a hat. Handle may cause discomfort."

MC1010

MC1002

MC1000

MC1012

MC1001

MC1005 - *front and side views*

MC1101

Premiums

MC1000	McBoo Bag, Witch, green, Week 1	1 - 2
MC1001	McBoo Bag, Ghost, purple, Week 2	1 - 2
MC1002	McBoo Bag, Monster, orange, Week 3	1 - 2
MC1003	Day Glo Pumpkin, *M* black handle	2 - 4
MC1004	Glow-in-the-Dark Ghost, *M* black handle	2 - 4
MC1005	Day Glo Witch, *M* black handle	2 - 4

Point of Purchase

MC1010	Translite, menu board	6 - 10
MC1011	Translite, drive-thru	4 - 8
MC1012	McBoo Ceiling Dangler, displayed 1 bag	2 - 5

McBUNNY PAILS, 1989

McBunny Pails were a regional Happy Meal which ran in the Chicago area in April 1989 and in other regions in 1990 and 1991. Each premium had 3 parts: pail, lid and handle. A bunny face was on the front of each pail and the bunny's name was on the back. The yellow handle was shaped like bunny ears – or its shape could be conceived as the McDonald's *M*.

Premiums

MC1101	Fluffy, white w/blue graphics, blue lid	3 - 5
MC1102	Pinky, white w/yellow graphics, yellow lid	3 - 5
MC1103	Whiskers, white w/green graphics, green lid	3 - 5

Point of Purchase

MC1105	Translite, menu board	8 - 10
MC1106	Translite, drive-thru	6 - 8

MC1102

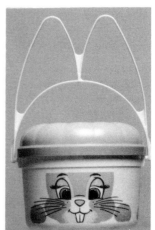

MC1103

McCHARACTERS ON BIKES, 1991

Towards the end of August 1991 when supplies of the Barbie/Hot Wheels premiums were depleted, some stores received McCharacters on bikes to use as fill-in premiums until the next scheduled Happy Meal. Each premium came in 4 pieces – the bike's front, middle and back plus a character. The card inside the package showed the bikes hooked together to form a "bicycle built for four". The Ronald and Hamburglar bikes were the same style and the Birdie and Grimace bikes matched. These bikes had been used in 1989 in the Muppet

MC1105

Kids Happy Meal. The four characters on bikes had previously been a promotion in Europe with four matching boxes. No boxes or point of purchase items were used in the United States.

Premiums

MC2001	Birdie, pink bike/blue wheels	3 - 7
MC2002	Grimace, blue bike/green wheels	3 - 7
MC2003	Hamburglar, yellow bike/red wheels	3 - 7
MC2004	Ronald, red bike, yellow wheels	3 - 7

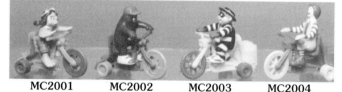

MC2001   MC2002   MC2003   MC2004

McDINO CHANGEABLES, 1991

McDonald's menu items which transformed into dinosaurs were the premiums for a Happy Meal May 24 – June 20, 1991. Two different transformers were offered each week. A bonus coupon book for over $12 in savings on well-known products came in some of the polybags. The "Under 3" premiums had no moveable parts and came in a zebra-stripped polybag.

Premiums

MC3000	Happy Meal-O-Don, Week 1	2 - 3
MC3001	Quarter Pounder with Cheese-O-Saur, Week 1	2 - 3
MC3002	Hot Cakes-O-Dactyl, Week 2	2 - 3
MC3003	McNuggets-O-Saurus, Week 2	2 - 3

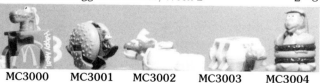

MC3000   MC3001   MC3002   MC3003   MC3004

MC3005   MC3006   MC3007   MC3008   MC3009

MC3022

MC3020

MC3004	Big Mac-O-Saurus Rex, Week 3	2 - 3
MC3005	Fry-Ceratops, Week 3	2 - 3
MC3006	McDino Cone, Week 4	2 - 3
MC3007	Tri-Shake-Atops, Week 4	2 - 3
MC3008	Bronto Cheeseburger (Under 3)	2 - 4
MC3009	Small Fry-Ceratops (Under 3)	2 - 4

Sack, 6" x 12"

MC3015	Two McDinos	1 - 2

Point of Purchase

MC3020	Translite, menu board	6 - 10
MC3021	Translite, drive-thru	4 - 8
MC3022	Counter Display w/premiums, motion	60 - 90

MC3015

Artist's conception of McDonaldland Craft Kit

MC4020

McDONALDLAND BAND, 1986

Band instruments embossed with McDonaldland characters were what attracted kids to the Apr 27 – June 4, 1987 regional Happy Meal. Eight band instruments, measuring 2 to 3" long, were featured during this 5-week run. The kazoo and siren whistle were repeated, so 2 instruments were offered per week. The train whistle and pan pipes were considered safe for children of all ages, thereby acceptable for the "Under 3" group. None of the instruments were polybagged. (**NOTE**: In 1992, the exact same kazoo, saxophone, siren whistle, boat whistle, train whistle and the pan pipes appeared in K-Mart stores on two blister packs under the title "Music Band" put out by Imperial Toy Corp.)

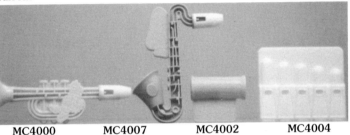

| MC4000 | MC4007 | MC4002 | MC4004 |
| MC4003 | MC4006 | MC4001 | MC4005 |

Premiums

MC4000	Trumpet, Fry Kid, green, Week 1	2 - 4
MC4001	Kazoo, Birdie, pink, Weeks 1 & 4	1 - 2
MC4002	Siren Whistle, Hamburglar, orange, Weeks 2 & 5	1 - 2
MC4003	Train Whistle, Ronald, purple, Week 2	1 - 2
MC4004	Pan Pipes, Ronald, yellow, Week 3	1 - 3
MC4005	Harmonica, Ronald, red, Week 3	2 - 4
MC4006	Boat Whistle, Fry Kid, blue, Week 4	1 - 2
MC4007	Saxophone, Grimace, purple, Week 5	1 - 3

Boxes

MC4010	Band Concert	1 - 3
MC4011	Can You Find?	1 - 3

MC4012	Jam Session	1 - 3
MC4013	Professor/Hamburglar	1 - 3

Point of Purchase

MC4020	Translite, menu board	6 - 10
MC4021	Translite, drive-thru	4 - 8
MC4022	Message Center Insert, cardboard	6 - 10

McDONALDLAND CRAFT KIT, 1990

An option for stores to use the premiums listed below was made during the "Open Window" time, Sept 7 – Oct 4, 1990. As of the date of publication, there has been no confirmation of these having been produced.

MC4010   MC4011   MC4012   MC4013

MC4500   MC4501   MC4502   MC4503

MC4504   MC4505   MC4506   MC4507

MC4510   MC4511

Premiums

Hamburglar Paintbrush & Paints		?
Grimace Tape Measure		?
Fry Guy Safety Scissors		?
McDonald's Adhesive Tape Dispenser		?
Grimace figure (Under 3)		?

McDONALDLAND DOUGH, 1990

Modeling compound came in the national option Happy Meal, Sept 7 to Oct 4, 1990. Two premiums were given out each week. Character molds were located inside the 2-oz cans of dough. The color of the can lid and the dough matched.

Premiums

MC4500	Red dough w/red Ronald star mold, Week 1	2 - 4
MC4501	Yellow dough w/red Ronald square mold, Week 1	2 - 4
MC4502	Green dough w/green Fry Girl octagon mold, Week 2	2 - 4
MC4503	Blue dough w/green Fry Guy hexagon mold, Week 2	2 - 4
MC4504	Purple dough w/purple Grimace square mold, Week 3	2 - 4
MC4505	Orange dough w/purple Grimace triangle mold, Week 3	2 - 4
MC4506	Pink dough w/yellow Birdie heart mold, Week 4	2 - 4
MC4507	White dough w/yellow Birdie circle mold, Week 4	2 - 4

Boxes

MC4510	Hoop to it!, orange	1 - 3
MC4511	Tic-Tac-Toe, green	1 - 3

Point of Purchase

MC4515	Translite, menu board	6 - 10
MC4516	Translite, drive-thru	4 - 8
MC4517	Menu Board Price Lug-On	2 - 4

McDONALDLAND EXPRESS, 1982

Four vacuform railroad cars made up the McDonaldland Express. The cars connected together to create a train. The premium served as the Happy Meal container. Each one was issued in 2 colors and came with a decal sheet. This national promotion ran June 11 – July 15, 1982. The recommendation

MC4515

MC4810

MC4803   MC4801

MC4802   MC4800

was made for each store to order more engines than the other cars. This enabled the purchaser who missed Week 1 to pick up the engine at any point in the time frame of this offering.

Premiums

MC4800	Engine, red or blue, Week 1	8 - 12
MC4801	Coach, blue or orange, Week 2	8 - 12
MC4802	Freight Car, green or orange, Week 3	8 - 12
MC4803	Caboose, green or red, Week 4	8 - 12
MC4804	Train car only	3 - 5
MC4805	Train car w/separate sticker sheet	10 - 15
MC4806	Sticker sheet only	4 - 6

Point of Purchase

MC4810	Translite, menu board/drive-thru (large)	10 - 15
MC4811	Message Center Insert, cardboard	10 - 15
MC4812	Counter Display w/premium of week, motion	75 - 100
MC4813	Ceiling Dangler w/4 cars	15 - 35
MC4814	Permanent Display Header Card	6 - 8

McDONALDLAND JUNCTION, 1983

A railroad theme was again featured during Jan 17 – Mar 27, 1983. Included with the McDonaldland Junction Happy Meal was the Winter '82/83 *McDonaldland Fun Times* magazine which featured trains. Each of the 4 plastic cars were issued in 2 colors with 1 color being more prevalent than the other. As the car moved a McDonaldland character bobbed up and down. The pieces for each car came on a plastic tree and had to be snapped off and assembled. The 6 boxes were designed as separate buildings and when put together, formed McDonaldland Junction.

MC4812

MC5401	MC5402	MC5404	MC5406

Premiums

MC5400	Ronald McDonald Engine, red, #1	2 - 6
MC5401	Ronald McDonald Engine, blue, #1	4 - 10
MC5402	Hamburger Patch Flatcar, green, #2	2 - 6
MC5403	Hamburger Patch Flatcar, white, #2	6 - 12
MC5404	Birdie Parlor Car, yellow, #3	2 - 6
MC5405	Birdie Parlor Car, pink, #3	4 - 10
MC5406	Grimace Caboose, purple, #4	2 - 6
MC5407	Grimace Caboose, orange, #4	4 - 10

Boxes

MC5410	Engine Barn	2 - 5
MC5411	Post Office	2 - 5
MC5412	Signal Tower	2 - 5
MC5413	Station	2 - 5
MC5414	Town Hall	2 - 5
MC5415	Train Tunnel	2 - 5

Point of Purchase

MC5420	Translite, menu board/drive-thru (large)	10 - 15
MC5421	Message Center Insert, cardboard	10 - 15
MC5422	Permanent Display Header Card	6 - 10
MC5423	Menu Board Lug-On	6 - 10

McDRIVE THRU CREW, 1990

McDrive Thru Crew appeared in 1990 as a clean-up set of toys. The 4 pull-back motorized vehicles featured menu item characters which could turn. Each premium came in a polybag with an insert card. Special containers or point of purchase displays are not known to have been produced.

MC5903	MC5900	MC5901	MC5902

Premiums

MC5900	Fries in Potato Speedster	3 - 7
MC5901	Hamburger in Catsup Racer	3 - 7
MC5902	McNugget in Egg Roadster	3 - 7
MC5903	Shake in Milk Carton Zoomer	3 - 7

MC5420

MC5410   MC5411   MC5412

MC5413   MC5414   MC5415

McNUGGET BUDDIES, 1988

Chicken McNugget characters were the basis for a national Happy Meal from Dec 30, 1988 to Jan 26, 1989. McNugget Buddies were a part of the McDonald's Saturday morning TV commercials. The 10 different characters each came with 3 interchangeable parts – body, hair or hat, and belt. One character, Corny, showed up with a belt in 2 different colors. The "Under 3" characters had no removable parts. Some premiums were polybagged with the information printed on the bag; while some came in a clear bag with an insert card. Two McNugget Buddies were featured each week.

Some stores also offered a "Dress–Up McNuggets" peel-off sheet. Various facial features and articles of clothing could be placed on McNugget body outlines to create different looks. This carried a 1988 McDonald's Corporation copyright.

MC7033

Premiums

MC7000	Cowpoke, Week 1	2 - 4
MC7001	First-Class, Week 1	2 - 4
MC7002	Sarge, Week 2	2 - 4
MC7003	Drummer, Week 2	2 - 4
MC7004	Corny, Week 3 (red popcorn belt)	2 - 4
MC7005	Corny, Week 3 (beige popcorn belt)	2 - 4
MC7006	Sparky, Week 3	2 - 4
MC7007	Boomerang, Week 4	2 - 4
MC7008	Volley, Week 4	2 - 4
MC7009	Snorkel, Week 5	2 - 4
MC7010	Rocker, Week 5	2 - 4
MC7011	Daisy (Under 3)	3 - 6
MC7012	Slugger (Under 3)	3 - 6
MC7013	Dress-Up McNuggets sheet	2 - 4

Boxes

MC7020	Apartments	1 - 3
MC7021	Beauty Shop	1 - 3
MC7022	Gardens	1 - 3
MC7023	Post Office	1 - 3

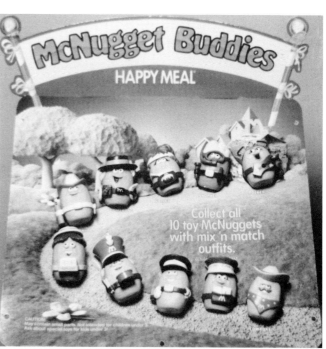

MC7032

MC7020 MC7021 MC7022 MC7023

MC7000-13

Point of Purchase

MC7030	Translite, menu board	6 - 10
MC7031	Translite, drive-thru	4 - 8
MC7032	Counter Display w/premiums	60 - 90
MC7033	Menu Board Premium Lug-On	6 - 10

METROZOO, 1987

A South Florida regional Happy Meal ran as a tie-in with the MetroZoo in Miami, FL during mid-Feb to mid-Mar 1987. The 4 animals were from the Bully Zoo Collection. The hard rubber animals were polybagged with a map giving the location of the MetroZoo.

Premiums

ME8001	Chimp, black w/tan face	10 - 20

MC7030

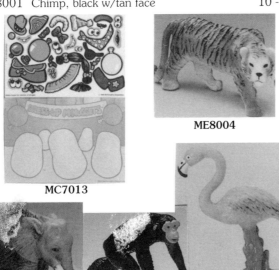

MC7013 ME8004

ME8020

ME8002 ME8001 ME8003

ME8015   MI1115   MI1116

ME8002	Elephant, gray w/white tusk	10 - 20
ME8003	Flamingo, pink w/yellow bill	10 - 20
ME8004	Tiger, white w/rust colored stripes	10 - 20
Box		
ME8015	MetroZoo	8 - 12
Point of Purchase		
ME8020	Translite, menu board	12 - 18
ME8021	Translite, drive-thru	10 - 12

MI1100   MI1101   MI1102   MI1103   MI1104

MICKEY'S BIRTHDAYLAND, 1988

Mickey's Birthdayland Happy Meal was based on the attraction at Walt Disney World in Orlando, FL. This was the first time McDonald's promoted the major Disney characters. The national promotion (Mar 17 – Apr 20, 1989) featured 5 Disney characters in motorized vehicles which ran and spun when pulled back and let go. The premiums for the "Under 3" age group were 4 cars imported from Sweden (Viking Toys) with moveable wheels. Two of the cars came in 2 different colors, thus 6 different "Under 3" premiums were available. All premiums were polybagged. Some of the polybags had the information printed directly on the bag; while some of the polybags were clear and an insert card was enclosed.

MI1127

Premiums

MI1100	Donald Duck, train engine, green, #1	2 - 4
MI1101	Minnie Mouse, convertible, pink, #2	2 - 4
MI1102	Goofy, jalopy, blue, #3	2 - 4
MI1103	Pluto, car w/rumble seat, purple, #4	2 - 4
MI1104	Mickey Mouse, roadster, red, #5	2 - 4
MI1105	Donald Duck, jeepster, blue or green (Under 3)	3 - 6
MI1106	Goofy, sedan, blue or green (Under 3)	3 - 6
MI1107	Mickey, roadster, red (Under 3)	3 - 6
MI1108	Minnie, convertible, pink (Under 3)	3 - 6
Boxes		
MI1115	Barn	1 - 3

MI1117   MI1118   MI1119

| MI1105 | MI1105 | MI1106 | MI1106 | MI1107 | MI1108 |

MI1116	Mickey's House	1 - 3
MI1117	Minnie's Dress Shop	1 - 3
MI1118	Theatre	1 - 3
MI1119	Train Station	1 - 3

Point of Purchase

MI1125	Translite, menu board	6 -1 0
MI1126	Translite, drive-thru	4 - 8
MI1127	Counter Display w/2 sets of premiums, motion	80 - 125
MI1128	Menu Board "Available Now" Lug-On, 1 for each premium, each	4 - 5

MIGHTY MINI 4x4, 1991/92

The West Coast ran a promotion featuring Mighty Mini 4x4 vehicles from Mar 8 – Apr 12, 1991 and several areas used this promotion during the Feb 7 – Mar 6, 1992 "Open Window". Four wind-up trucks were activated by turning the crank extending from them. A larger sized truck of 1-piece design was the "Under 3" offering. Each premium came in a polybag with an insert card. During the 1992 offering, a sack replaced the box.

Premiums

MI5000	Dune Buster (Baja Bug), pink, #1	1 - 3
M5001	Li'l Classic ('57 Thunderbird), yellow, #2	1 - 3
MI5002	Cargo Climber (Sport Van), orange, #3	1 - 3
MI5003	Pocket Pick-up, red, #4	1 - 3
MI5004	Pocket Pick-up, blue (Under 3)	1 - 4

| MI5000 | MI5001 | MI5002 | MI5003 | MI5004 |

Box/Sack

| MI5010 | Four Mini's box | 1 - 3 |
| MI5011 | Mighty Mini 4x4 paper sack, 6" x 12" | 1 - 2 |

Point of Purchase

| MI5015 | Translite, menu board | 6 - 10 |
| MI5016 | Translite, drive-thru | 4 - 8 |

MINIFLEXIES (See GENERIC, 1979)

MI5011

MI5015

MI1125

MI5010

MIX 'EM UP MONSTERS, 1989/90

Four monsters with 3 interchangeable parts (body, head, tail) were made by Current, Inc. for this regional Happy Meal which ran in Jan and Oct 1989 and again in 1990. By interchanging the parts, 64 different monsters could be created.

Premiums

MI9000	Bibble, green (extended eyes)	3 - 5
MI9001	Corkle, blue (folded arms)	3 - 5
MI9002	Gropple, yellow (2 heads)	3 - 5
MI9003	Thugger, purple (large tusks)	3 - 5

Box

| MI9010 | Monsters on Moon | 1 - 4 |

MI9010

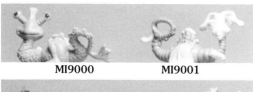

MI9000   MI9001

MI9002   MI9003

Point of Purchase

| MI9015 | Translite, menu board | 6 - 10 |
| MI9016 | Translite, drive-thru | 4 - 8 |

MI9015

MOVEABLES, 1988

The St. Louis region did McDonald character figures in a "Moveables" Happy Meal in 1988. The figures themselves are "bendies", but the small size doesn't allow much movement. Each figure came in a printed polybag with "Safety tested for children age 3 and over. Caution: May contain small parts not intended for children under 3. Made in China".

Premiums

MO8900	Birdie	3 - 8
MO8901	Captain	3 - 8
MO8902	Fry Girl	3 - 8

MO8904   MO8905   MO8901

MO8900   MO8902   MO8903

MO8903	Hamburglar	3 - 8
MO8904	Professor	3 - 8
MO8905	Ronald	3 - 8

Box

| MO8910 | Ship | 1 - 5 |

Point of Purchase

| MO8915 | Translite, menu board | 8 - 12 |
| MO8916 | Translite, drive-thru | 6 - 10 |

MO8910

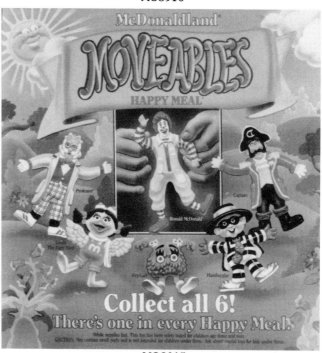

MO9015

MUPPET BABIES, 1986, Test

Muppet Babies were tested in Savannah, GA from Aug 8 to Sept 7, 1986. The card inside the package with each of the 4 characters and the mode of transportation they could be placed on or in was printed in a different color. Gonzo and Miss Piggy were changed for the national run.

Premiums

MU6000	Gonzo, suspenders cross in back, no shoes, green Big Wheel, blue pkg, Set 1	10 - 20
MU6001	Fozzie, yellow horse, orange pkg, Set 2	10 - 20
MU6002	Miss Piggy, pink car, pink ribbon bow flat against hair, green pkg, Set 3	10 - 20
MU6003	Kermit, red skateboard, red pkg, Set 4	10 - 20

MUPPET BABIES, 1987

Jim Henson's Muppet Babies first appeared during a flash-

MU6001   MU6000   MU6003   MU6002

back sequence in the 1984 movie *The Muppets Take Manhattan*. That fall, a Muppet Babies cartoon series began on CBS Saturday morning TV. The national Happy Meal (June 5 – July 9, 1987) featured the 4 Muppet characters on moving wheel vehicles. For the "Under 3" group 2 figures of 1-piece design were offered. All came polybagged with insert card. The boxes contained punch-outs for the figures: for Kermit and Fozzie, costume additives; for Miss Piggy, a boat; for Gonzo, a horse.

Premiums

MU6021	Gonzo w/green trike, Set 1	1 - 3
MU6022	Fozzie w/yellow rocking horse, Set 2	1 - 3
MU6023	Miss Piggy w/pink car, bow on dress, Set 3	1 - 3
MU6024	Kermit w/red skateboard, Set 4	1 - 3
MU6025	Kermit on skates (Under 3)	2 - 4
MU6026	Miss Piggy on skates (Under 3)	2 - 4

Boxes

MU6030	Fozzie	1 - 3
MU6031	Gonzo	1 - 3
MU6032	Kermit	1 - 3
MU6033	Miss Piggy	1 - 3

MU6021   MU6022   MU6023   MU6024   MU6025   MU6026

Point of Purchase

MU6040	Translite, menu board	6 - 10
MU6041	Translite, drive-thru	4 - 8
MU6042	Counter Display w/premiums	60 - 90
MU6043	Register Topper	3 - 4

MUPPET BABIES, 1988 (See STORYBOOK MUPPET BABIES, 1988)

MUPPET BABIES, 1991/92

The Chicago region ran another Muppet Babies Happy Meal

MU6042

MU6033

MU6030   MU6031   MU6032

MU6040

MU6515

from Mar 8 – Apr 12, 1991. It was also used in the Feb 1992 Open Window in WI. The 4 vehicles were made to hook together. All premiums were polybagged with an insert card and placed in a sack.

Premiums
MU6500	Fozzie w/red wagon	3 - 5
MU6501	Gonzo w/green airplane	3 - 5
MU6502	Kermit w/yellow racer	3 - 5
MU6503	Miss Piggy w/blue tricycle	3 - 5

Sack
MU6510	Race, full-color	1 - 3

Point of Purchase
MU6515	Translite, menu board	8 - 10
MU6516	Translite, drive-thru	6 - 8

MUPPET KIDS, 1989, Test

Springfield, MO area tested a Muppet Kids Happy Meal during the summer of 1989. This idea of "kids" was not continued by Jim Henson, so the promotion did not go beyond the test market. Each Muppet Kid and 4-piece bike (body, handle bars, front wheel, back wheel) came polybagged with an insert card. By using all 4 bodies, 1 front wheel and 1 back wheel, a bicycle for 4 could be built. For the "Under 3" premiums, the storybooks offered in the winter of 1988 were again used. (See STORYBOOK MUPPET BABIES, 1988)

Premiums
MU6800	Kermit, red bike w/yellow front wheel, Set 1	8 - 20
MU6801	Miss Piggy, pink bike w/green front wheel, Set 2	8 - 20
MU6802	Gonzo, yellow bike w/pink front wheel, Set 3	8 - 20
MU6803	Fozzie, green bike w/red front wheel, Set 4	8 - 20

MU6502   MU6503   MU6500   MU6501

MU6800   MU6801   MU6802   MU6803

MU6510

MU6810

MU6811

101

MU6815

MU6817

Boxes		
MU6810	Club House	2 - 10
MU6811	School	2 - 10
Point of Purchase		
MU6815	Translite, menu board	15 - 20
MU6816	Translite, drive-thru	12 - 15
MU6817	Counter Display w/premiums	125 - 175

MUSIC, 1985

A tie-in with Fisher-Price Toy Company's 33¹/₃ rpm records was featured in a Kansas City region promotion in Aug. 1985. Side A contained songs; the flip side contained a story. The 4 records came with a dust jacket. The back of the jacket included a $1 rebate coupon toward Fisher-Price purchases. The color of the record label and the dust jacket matched.

MU7510

Premiums

MU7500	Blue – Side A: If You're Happy/Little Bunny Foo Foo; Side B: The Ronald McDonald One-Man Band	2 - 6
MU7501	Green – Side A: She'll be Comin' Round the Mountain/Head, Shoulders, Knees, Toes; Side B: The Object is Music	2 - 6
MU7502	Pink – Side A: Boom, Boom, Ain't It Great to be Crazy?/Do Your Ears Hang Low?; Side B: The Music Machine	2 - 6
MU7503	Yellow – Side A: Do The Hokey Pokey/ Eensy, Weensy Spider; Side B: The Ronald McDonald Orchestra	2 - 6

Boxes

MU7510	Audience Clapping	2 - 5
MU7511	Can You Find?	2 - 5
MU7512	Jam Session	2 - 5
MU7513	Ronald Directing Band	2 - 5
Point of Purchase		
MU7520	Translite, menu board/drive-thru (large)	10 - 15
MU7521	Message Center Insert	10 - 15

MY LITTLE PONY (See TRANSFORMERS/MY LITTLE PONY, 1985)

MYSTERY, 1983

A mystery theme was highlighted in a Mar 28 - June 5, 1983 Happy Meal. Some stores used generic premiums or sub-

A Fisher-Price Record with each Happy Meal! Collect all Four.

MU7520

| MU7511 | MU7512 | MU7513 |

| MU7502 | MU7501 | MU7500 | MU7503 |

MY8001   MY8003

MY8000

stituted the Spring 1983 *McDonaldland Fun Times* magazine. Various colors and McDonald characters were featured in the 4 mystery related items, making a total of 15 premiums if all were available. The Crystal Ball may have been pulled during the production stage due to its inability to meet safety standards.

Premiums

MY8000 Detective Kit – Ronald McDonald kit   5 - 15
came w/case, tweezers, instruction sheet
for secret messages & rubbing finger paint.
Kit came in blue, orange and green on a
tree , #1

MY8001 Crystal Ball – a 2-piece plastic ball which   20 - 40
included a paper cube w/answers of *It's
Possible*; *Yes*; *Try Again*; *Robbie, Robbie*;
Maybe; *No* One end of ball was clear &
when turned over the answer would
appear. Pressed into the end of the ball
was a small face of Ronald or Big Mac or
Mayor McCheese. Came in pale yellow
or semi-clear, #2

MY8002 Magni-Finder – 3-piece magnifying   5 - 15
glass on a plastic tree. Imprinted on top
piece was face of Ronald, Early Bird or
French Fry Guys, #3

MY8003 Unpredict-a-Ball – 2 pieces on a plastic   5 - 15
tree. When rolled the ball goes straight;
twist it and it rolls another way. Came in
red, yellow or blue w/imprint of Ronald's
face, #4

Boxes

MY8010	Dog–Gone Mystery	2 - 6
MY8011	Golden Key	2 - 6
MY8012	Mysterious Map	2 - 6
MY8013	Ocean's Away!	2 - 6
MY8014	Thump, Blam, Bump Mystery	2 - 6

Point of Purchase

MY8020	Translite, menu board/drive-thru (large)	10 - 15
MY8021	Message Center Insert, cardboard	10 - 15
MY8022	Permanent Display Header Card	4 - 6
MY8023	Menu Board Premium Lug-On	4 - 6

MY8002 (Ronald)   MY8002 (Birdie)   MY8002 (Fry Guy)

| MY8011 | MY8012 | MY8013 |

MY8014   MY8010   MY8517

MYSTERY OF THE LOST ARCHES, 1992

The 4 premiums for this national Happy Meal, Jan 3–31, 1992 were toys which became other items. The camera became a multi-image lens; the cassette, a magnifier; the phone, a periscope; and the flashlight, a telescope. All toys were polybagged with an insert card.

After the first week during which the camera was issued, the McDonald's Corporation recalled all the cameras remaining in the stores. Children were getting their fingers caught in the hole in the back of the camera.

The "Under 3" premium was also the camera. Differences between the regular camera and this offering involved: 1) the sticker on the front which read "Search Team" was white instead of silver; 2) the "Under 3" type wrapper with the black and white zebra stripes around the insert paper was used with "Under 3 toy" printed in the lower right corner. The "Under 3" cameras were also recalled after the first week.

MY8503   MY8504   MY8505

Premiums

MY8501	Magic Lens Camera, blue/yellow, Week 1	2 - 6
MY8502	Micro-Cassette/Magnifier, green, Week 2	1 - 3
MY8503	Phone/Periscope, orange, Week 3	1 - 3
MY8504	Flashlight/Telescope, red/blue, Week 4	1 - 3
MY8505	Magic Lens Camera, white label (Under 3)	2 - 6

Sack, 6" x 12", paper

MY8510	Ronald/Pyramids, white w/color graphics	1 - 3

MY8510

MY8501   MY8502

Point of Purchase

MY8515	Translite, menu board	8 - 12
MY8516	Translite, drive-thru	6 - 8
MY8517	Tray Liner	1 -

MY8020

MY8515

GET THIS MODEL TODAY!
AVAILABLE IN 4 COLORS

McDonald's
SPACESHIP
HAPPY MEAL
4 different spaceships,
each in 4 different colors.

HAPPY MEAL includes a regular size hamburger or cheeseburger, regular size order of fries, regular size soft drink, and a decorative sheet of decals

McDonald's
BERENSTAIN BEARS
HAPPY MEAL
Collect
all 4
while supplies last!

CAUTION: May contain small parts. Not intended for children under 3.
Ask about special toys for kids under 3.

Potato Head
KIDS
HAPPY • MEAL

PLAYSKOOL

Collect all 12!

McDonald's
Little Travelers
Happy Meal
with LEGO
Building Sets

McDonald's
TURBO MACS
HAPPY MEAL

COLLECT ALL 4! One in each Turbo Macs
Happy Meal

NEW FOOD
Changeables
Happy Meal

COLLECT
ALL 8
FOR A
GALACTIC
ROBOT TEAM!

Fry-bot   Robo-cakes   Turbo Cone   Galacta Burger   Krypto Cup

CAUTION: May contain small parts.
Not intended for children under 3.
Alternate toys available for children under 3.

Walt Disney World
MICKEY'S BIRTHDAYLAND
Happy Meal

Meet Mickey in a
whole new land in the
Magic Kingdom!

Pull 'em
back and watch
'em go!

MICKEY'S PARTY

Collect
all 5 racers
while supplies last.

CAUTION: May contain small parts. Not intended for children under 3!
ASK ABOUT SPECIAL TOYS FOR KIDS UNDER 3!

McDonald's
Make waves with
ShipShape
HAPPY MEAL

THIS
WEEK'S
BOAT

Collect all 4!
$170 each
With Hamburger
$180 each
With Cheeseburger

They really float!

McDonald's presents
Walt Disney's Classic
101
DALMATIANS
HAPPY MEAL

COLLECT ALL 4 POSEABLE TOYS
While supplies last

Safety-tested for children of all ages. Recommended for children age 1 and over

LOOK FOR THE
IN THEATERS EVERY

Don't Monkey Around!

McDonald's
Safari Adventure Meal

With Hamburger.......$1.44 each
With Cheeseburger.....$1.54 each
*Plus tax (suggested retail price) While supply lasts.

includes:
• Regular size Hamburger or
  Cheeseburger (slight additional charge)
• Regular size order of French Fries
• Regular size Soft Drink
• McDonaldland Cookie Sampler

MATCHBOX ⓈSUPER GT HAPPY MEAL

COLLECT ALL 16!

1 Matchbox® Super GT Car In Each Happy Meal®

While supplies last. This toy has been safety tested for children age 3 and over. CAUTION: May contain small parts and is not intended for children under 3. Ask about special items for children under age 3.

ASTROSNIKS

HAPPY MEAL®

Receive an Astrosnik™
character with each
Happy Meal® purchased.
While supplies last.

McDonald's
Funny Fry Friends
Happy Meal

Change 'em around

Collect all 8, while supplies last.
CAUTION: May contain small parts. Not intended for children under 3.
Ask about special toys for kids under 3.

Remember your favorite books as a child?

Little Golden Book
HAPPY MEAL

Nintendo SUPER MARIO 3 BROS. HAPPY MEAL

Koopa Paratroopa Hops!

Luigi Zooms Around!

Little Goomba Flips!

Super Mario Jumps!

COLLECT ALL 4 ACTION TOYS!
WHILE SUPPLIES LAST.
CAUTION: May contain small parts. Not intended for children under 3.
Ask about the special toy for kids under 3.

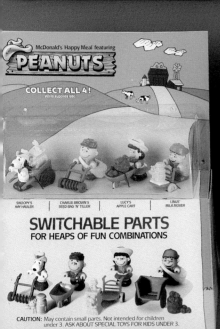

McDonald's Happy Meal featuring
PEANUTS

COLLECT ALL 4!
While supplies last.

| SNOOPY'S HAY HAULER | CHARLIE BROWN'S SEED BAG 'N' TILLER | LUCY'S APPLE CART | LINUS' MILK MOVER |

SWITCHABLE PARTS
FOR HEAPS OF FUN COMBINATIONS

CAUTION: May contain small parts. Not intended for children under 3. ASK ABOUT SPECIAL TOYS FOR KIDS UNDER 3.

Walt Disney's Classic
THE JUNGLE BOOK
HAPPY MEAL

LOOK FOR THE MOVIE NOW IN THEATERS EVERYWHERE!

Shere Khan pounces!

Baloo dances!

King Louie somersaults!

Kaa rocks his head!

Collect all 4 windup toys!
While supplies last.

CAUTION: May contain small parts. Not intended for children under 3. Ask about special toys for kids under 3.

McDonald's Happy Meal featuring
Jim Henson's
MUPPET BABIES

Collect all 4!
(while supplies last)

CAUTION: May contain small parts. Not intended for children under 3. Ask about special toys for kids under 3!

McDonald's
STAR TREK MEAL

5 NEW BOXES! 5 STAR TREK PRIZES!

With Hamburger .... $1.30 EACH
With Cheeseburger .... $1.35 EACH

INCLUDES:
• A Regular size Hamburger ...or Cheeseburger (slight additional charge)
• Regular size order of French Fries • Regular size Soft Drink
• McDonaldland Cookie Sampler and a Star Trek prize!

Offer ends February 3, 1980 or while supply lasts.

Hot Wheels®
MATTEL

HAPPY MEAL

Available NOW

COLLECT ALL 12
One in each Hot Wheels
Happy Meal

While supplies last. This toy has been safety tested for children age 3 and over.
CAUTION: May contain small parts and is not intended for children under
3 years of age. Ask about special toys for kids under 3.

McDonald's Happy Meal featuring
Jim Henson's
FRAGGLE ROCK

Boober & Wembley Fraggle

Collect all 4

CAUTION: May contain small parts. Not intended for children under 3.
Ask about special toys for kids under 3!

McDonald's Happy Meal
FEATURING
Jim Henson's
MUPPET KIDS

THE MORE THE BETTER
TO SNAP TOGETHER
WHILE SUPPLIES LAST.

CAUTION: May contain small parts. Not intended for children under 3.
ASK ABOUT SPECIAL ITEMS FOR KIDS UNDER 3!

McDonald's
HAPPY MEAL
featuring

TINY TOON
Adventures

There's a different car and driver on the flip side.
Collect all 4, and get all 8!

FLIP CARS

while supplies last

McDonald's Happy Meal presents
LEGO MOTION
COLLECT ALL 8 BUILDING SETS WHILE SUPPLIES LAST.

CAUTION: LEGO Building Sets contain small parts
and are not intended for children under 3.

McDonald's
Sport Ball
HAPPY MEAL

Catch 'em all!
while supplies last.

Basketball and hoop are safety-tested for children age 3 and over.
CAUTION: May contain small parts. Not intended for children under 3.
Ask about special toys for kids under 3!

ALL ABOARD!

McDonaldLAND EXPRESS
HAPPY MEAL

THIS WEEK'S CAR

COLLECT
ALL 4 CARS

HAPPY MEAL INCLUDES:
• regular size Hamburger or
Cheeseburger
• regular size order of fries
• regular size soft drink
• decals featuring
McDonaldland characters

McDINO
CHANGEABLES
HAPPY MEAL

Happy Meal

COLLECT
ALL 8
While supplies last.

Safety-tested for children age 3 and over. CAUTION: May contain small parts.
Not intended for children under 3. Ask about special toys for kids under 3.

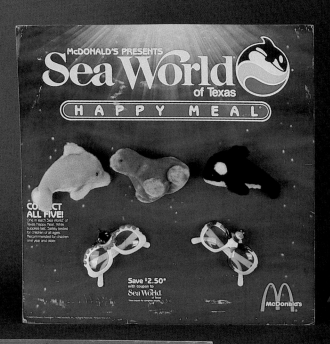

McDONALD'S PRESENTS
Sea World
of Texas
HAPPY MEAL

COLLECT
ALL FIVE!
One in each Sea World of
Texas Happy Meal. While
supplies last. Safety tested
for children of all ages.
Recommended for children
one year and older.

Save $2.50*
with coupon to
Sea World
of Texas
*See coupon for complete details.

McDonald's

Mac Tonight

Travel Toys
One in every Happy Meal*

Collect All Six
While supplies last.

CAUTION: May contain small parts. Not intended for children under 3.
Ask about special toys for kids under 3.
Jeep® is a registered trademark of Jeep Eagle Corporations.

McDonald's HAPPY MEAL starring

Hot Wheels
MATTEL

ASK FOR A CAR OR A FIGURINE.
Collect them all while supplies last.

CAUTION: May contain small parts. Not intended for children under 3. ASK ABOUT SPECIAL TOYS FOR KIDS UNDER 3.

Barbie

Barbie
with
glamorous
play scene

McDonald's
I Like Bikes
HAPPY   MEAL

BIRDIE
SPINNER

FRY GUY
HORN

GRIMACE
REARVIEW
REFLECTOR

...ONALD
...LE BASKET

CAUTION: May contain small parts.
Not intended for children under 3.
ASK ABOUT THE SPECIAL TOY
FOR KIDS UNDER 3.

Collect All 4
While supplies last.

McDonald's Happy Meal With

ALVIN & CHIPMUNKS

Collect All 4!
While supplies last.
One in each Happy Meal.

CAUTION: May contain small
parts and is not intended for
children under age 3. Ask
about special toys
for kids under 3.

McDonald's

⊙ TARGET
coupon
available here
and inside
each
Happy Meal

McDonald's Happy Meal featuring
GARFIELD

Collect 'em all...You can never get enough of me!
While supplies last.

CAUTION: May contain small parts.
Not intended for children under 3.
ASK ABOUT SPECIAL TOYS FOR KIDS UNDER 3!

Disney's
Available
Now
CHIP 'N DALE
RESCUE RANGERS
HAPPY MEAL

Make hundreds of Gadgetmobiles with mix 'n match parts!

Chip's Whirly-Copter   Dale's Roto-Roadster   Gadget's Rescue Racer   Monterey Jack's Propel-A-Phone

Look for "Chip 'N Dale Rescue Rangers"
on TV every weekday afternoon.

CAUTION: May contain small parts. Not intended for children under 3. ASK ABOUT SPECIAL TOYS FOR KIDS UNDER 3.

McDonald's presents
Disney's
TALESPIN
HAPPY MEAL

COLLECT
ALL 4
DIE-CAST PLANES
while supplies last

Wildcat's Flying Machine   Baloo's Seaplane   Molly's Biplane   Kit's Racing Plane

Look for
"Tale Spin"
on TV every
weekday afternoon

CAUTION: May contain small parts. Alternate items
available for children under 3.

NATURE'S HELPERS, 1991

Nature's Helpers Happy Meal ran on a national basis from Apr 13 – May 16, 1991. The promotion coincided with McDonald's Let's Get Growing America tree giveaway program. An environmental brochure came with each spring-related item. The seeds were from the Burpee Company. The Double Digger, Bird Feeder, Rack, and "Under 3" Rack were polybagged with an insert card.

Premiums

NA8000	Double Digger (green) w/cucumber seeds & "Why are there trees & vegetables?" Hole digger came apart to make 2 shovels, #1	1 - 3
NA8001	3-pc Bird Feeder (clear-orange-green) & "Why are there birds?", #2	1 - 3
NA8002	Watering Can (blue) & "Why are there flowers?", #3	1 - 3
NA8003	2-pc Terrarium (green base w/dome) & "How does the world work?", #4	1 - 3
NA8004	Rake (yellow) w/marigold seeds & "How does your garden grow?", #5	1 - 3
NA8005	Same as NA8004 w/o the seeds (Under 3)	– - 6

NA8015

NA8010

NA8003   NA8004

NA8002   NA8000   NA8001

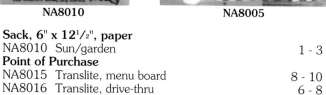

NE8000 NE8001 NE8002 NE8003 NE8004 NE8005

NA8005

Sack, 6" x 12¹/₂", paper

NA8010	Sun/garden	1 - 3

Point of Purchase

NA8015	Translite, menu board	8 - 10
NA8016	Translite, drive-thru	6 - 8

Box

NE8010	Archies/Fun Park	4 - 7

Point of Purchase

NE8015	Translite, menu board	10 - 15
NE8016	Translite, drive-thru	8 - 12

NEW ARCHIES, 1988

From the Archie comic book series came the New Archies Happy Meal in the St. Louis region in the spring of 1988. Six Archie character bumper cars with wheels, a yellow *M* inside a red circle on the front of the car and the McDonald's name on the bottom came in polybags printed with "Safety tested for children age 3 and over. Caution: May contain small parts not intended for children under 3. Made in China. ©1987 Archie Comic Publications, Inc., ™ and ® Designate Trademarks of the Archie Comic Publications, Inc. and are used, under license, by Prime Designs, Ltd." A variation has been noted involving the lack of the McDonald's name and the yellow *M* is not within a red circle.

Premiums

NE8000	Archie, red car	4 - 8
NE8001	Betty, blue car	4 - 8
NE8002	Jughead, yellow car	4 - 8
NE8003	Moose, pink car	4 - 8
NE8004	Reggie, green car	4 - 8
NE8005	Veronica, purple car	4 - 8

NEW FOOD CHANGEABLES, 1989

Food items which changed into robots became a national promotion from May 19 – June 15, 1989. Six of the 8 premiums (2 per week) were new designs never used before. The

NE8010

hands and feet of these premiums were painted. All came in polybags with an insert card except the "Under 3" bag had the writing printed on it. The "Under 3" premium was a Rubik's cube design of 3 pieces featuring the head, body, and feet of the 4 characters (Birdie, Grimace, CosMc, Hamburglar) shown 1 on each side of the cube.

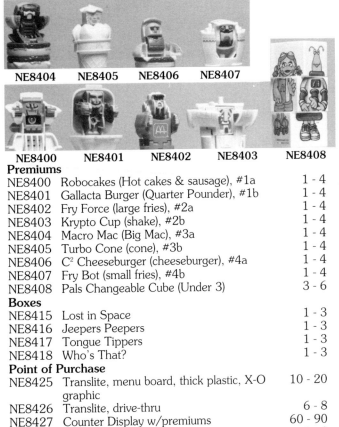

NE8404   NE8405   NE8406   NE8407

NE8400   NE8401   NE8402   NE8403   NE8408

Premiums

NE8400	Robocakes (Hot cakes & sausage), #1a	1 - 4
NE8401	Gallacta Burger (Quarter Pounder), #1b	1 - 4
NE8402	Fry Force (large fries), #2a	1 - 4
NE8403	Krypto Cup (shake), #2b	1 - 4
NE8404	Macro Mac (Big Mac), #3a	1 - 4
NE8405	Turbo Cone (cone), #3b	1 - 4
NE8406	C² Cheeseburger (cheeseburger), #4a	1 - 4
NE8407	Fry Bot (small fries), #4b	1 - 4
NE8408	Pals Changeable Cube (Under 3)	3 - 6

Boxes

NE8415	Lost in Space	1 - 3
NE8416	Jeepers Peepers	1 - 3
NE8417	Tongue Tippers	1 - 3
NE8418	Who's That?	1 - 3

Point of Purchase

NE8425	Translite, menu board, thick plastic, X-O graphic	10 - 20
NE8426	Translite, drive-thru	6 - 8
NE8427	Counter Display w/premiums	60 - 90
NE8428	Menu Board Premium Lug-On	6 - 8

NE8427

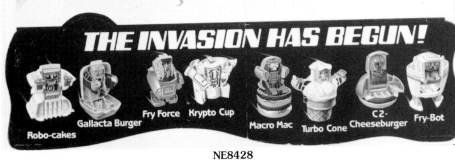

NE8428

NE8415

NE8416   NE8417   NE8418

114

NE8426

OLD McDONALD'S (See BARNYARD, 1986)

OLD WEST, 1981

Western town buildings were the focus in a national option program in the spring of 1981. The McDonald's Corporation developed the boxes which could all be used to create a western town named "Hamburger Gulch". Each market was allowed to decide the premiums to be used. It is difficult to know what was used in every market. Some markets used Diener Company hard rubber figures. They all came in blue, brown, orange, or yellow.

OL4121

Premiums

OL4100	Indian Squaw, hands crossed	6 - 8
OL4101	Indian Brave, face to side	6 - 8
OL4102	Cowgirl w/gun	6 - 8
OL4103	Cowboy, being held up	6 - 8
OL4104	Sheriff, hands on side	6 - 8
OL4105	Woodsman, knife in hand	6 - 8

Boxes

OL4110	Blacksmith Shop	4 - 12
OL4111	General Store	4 - 12
OL4112	Hotel	4 - 12

OL4110   OL4111   OL4112

OL4113   OL4114   OL4115

OL4102 OL4100 OL4103 OL4105 OL4104 OL4101

OL4821

OL4113	Music Hall	4 - 12
OL4114	Sheriff's Office	4 - 12
OL4115	Train Depot	4 - 12
Point of Purchase		
OL4120	Translite, menu board/drive-thru (large)	10 - 15
OL4121	Message Center Insert, cardboard	10 - 15

OLIVER & CO., 1988

Oliver, a new Walt Disney Studio picture, provided the tie-in for the 1988 holiday season (Nov 25 – Dec 29). The movie is based on the Charles Dickens book *Oliver Twist*. Four *Oliver* characters became soft rubber finger puppets in this exclusive to McDonald's. All were polybagged with an insert card.

Premiums

OL4400	Oliver, spunky street kitten, Set 1	1 - 4
OL4401	Francis, an aspiring actor bulldog, Set 2	1 - 4
OL4402	Georgette, a former French poodle beauty queen, Set 3	1 - 4
OL4403	Dodger, the coolest dog on the streets, Set 4	1 - 4

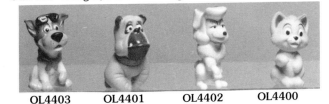

OL4403   OL4401   OL4402   OL4400

Boxes

OL4410	Funny Bones	1 - 3
OL4411	Noisy Neighborhood	1 - 3
OL4412	Shadow Scramble	1 - 3
OL4413	Tricky Trike	1 - 3
Point of Purchase		
OL4420	Translite, menu board	6 - 10
OL4421	Translite, drive-thru	4 - 8

OLYMPIC BEACH BALL (See BEACH BALL – OLYMPIC, 1984)

OLYMPIC SPORTS, 1984

The Olympic Games was the tie-in for this national Happy Meal promotion, June 18 – Aug 20, 1984. Five McDonald's

OL4420

Olympic "Guess n' Glow" puzzles were created. Each polybagged 4³/₄" x 3³/₄" puzzle featured McDonald characters in an olympic event with one character which glowed in the dark – the answer to the riddle.

Premiums

OL4800	Guess which guy comes in under the wire (track meet), Grimace/Hamburglar –	5 - 10

OL4804   OL4803

OL4410   OL4411   OL4412   OL4413

OL4811   OL4810   OL4812

OL4813   OL4814

OL4822

OL4800   OL4801   OL4802

	Fry Guy glow character	
OL4801	Guess who finished smiles ahead (bicycle race), Hamburglar/Birdie – Ronald glow character	5 - 10
OL4802	Guess who makes the biggest splash (diving contest), Captain/Birdie/Ronald – Grimace glow character	5 - 10
OL4803	Guess who stole the winning goal (soccer), Grimace/Fry Guy – Hamburglar glow character	5 - 10
OL4804	Who do you know that can help them row? (rowing contest), Ronald/Fry Guy – The Captain glow character	5 - 10

Boxes

OL4810	Boats Afloat	2 - 5
OL4811	In the Swim	2 - 5
OL4812	Just for Kicks	2 - 5
OL4813	Making Tracks	2 - 5
OL4814	Pedal Power	2 - 5

Point of Purchase

OL4820	Translite, menu board/drive-thru (large)	10 - 15
OL4821	Menu Board Premium Lug-On	6 - 8
OL4822	Permanent Display Header Card	6 - 8
OL4823	Message Center Insert, cardboard	10 - 15

OLYMPIC SPORTS, 1988

McDonald's again featured the Olympics in a Sept 9 – 29,

OL4820

1988 promotion. A national option program which was not used in all markets. Six 2" plastic medallions featured the McDonaldland characters in Olympic events. The front of the medallion is embossed with a 3-dimensional scene and the back of the pin has a tension clip to hook onto clothing.

Premiums

OL4850	Hamburglar/Hurdles, Week 1	3 - 6

OL4865

ON5502   ON5503

ON5504   ON5501

ON5505

Premiums

ON5501	On the Road to McDonald's Bead Game, green, 6-sided	4 - 8
ON5502	Hamburglar/Red Race Car On the Go Magic Slate	4 - 8
ON5503	Ronald/Yellow Car On the Go Magic Slate	4 - 8
ON5504	Stop and Go Bead Game, Hamburglar/ Ronald at Stop Light	4 - 8
ON5505	Transfers and City Scene Sheet, polybagged	5 - 10

Boxes

ON5510	Bridge	2 - 4
ON5511	Drive Thru	2 - 4
ON5512	Garage	2 - 4
ON5513	Tunnel	2 - 4

Point of Purchase

ON5520	Translite, menu board/drive-thru (large)	8 - 12
ON5521	Translite, drive-thru (small)	6 - 10

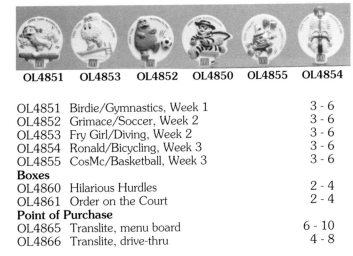

OL4851   OL4853   OL4852   OL4850   OL4855   OL4854

OL4851	Birdie/Gymnastics, Week 1	3 - 6
OL4852	Grimace/Soccer, Week 2	3 - 6
OL4853	Fry Girl/Diving, Week 2	3 - 6
OL4854	Ronald/Bicycling, Week 3	3 - 6
OL4855	CosMc/Basketball, Week 3	3 - 6

Boxes

OL4860	Hilarious Hurdles	2 - 4
OL4861	Order on the Court	2 - 4

Point of Purchase

OL4865	Translite, menu board	6 - 10
OL4866	Translite, drive-thru	4 - 8

ON THE GO, 1985

A travel theme highlighted the On the Go regional Happy Meal in 1985. All 5 travel related premiums were paper items.

ON THE GO, 1988

Another Happy Meal with the same title, "On the Go", ran on a national basis, Aug 12 – Sept 8, 1988. Rather than the 1985 travel theme, this time "On the Go" meant "Back to School." Two plastic lunch boxes with stickers and 2 vinyl lunch bags were the premiums. The plastic lunch boxes featured a school bulletin board for sticker usage and the other side was a molded McDonaldland "Back to School" scene. A different color lunch box with a school room scene sticker sheet already applied was the alternate premium for "Under 3."

OL4860   OL4861   ON5510

ON5511   ON5512   ON5513

ON5520

ON5616

         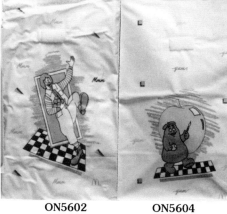

ON5601   ON5603   ON5605

ON5602   ON5604

Premiums

ON5601	Red lunch box, Week 1	2 - 4
ON5602	Yellow lunch bag, Ronald, Week 2	2 - 4
ON5603	Green lunch box, Week 3	2 - 4
ON5604	Blue lunch bag, Grimace, Week 4	2 - 4
ON5605	Blue lunch box (Under 3)	2 - 5
ON5606	ON5601 & ON5603 Lunch Box only	1 - 2
ON5607	ON5601 & ON5603 Lunch Box sheet w/separate sticker	3 - 5
ON5608	ON5601 & ON5603 Sticker Sheet only	1 - 2

Point of Purchase

ON5615	Translite, menu board	6 - 10
ON5616	Translite, drive-thru	4 - 8

101 DALMATIANS, 1991

This national promotion, July 5 – Aug 1, 1991, coincided with the re-release of the 1961 Walt Disney children's classic movie, *101 Dalmatians*. The four premiums were poseable figures and were issued in a polybag with the information printed on the bag. Four boxes of a new smaller shape were used.

Premiums

ON5700	Pongo, large Dalmatian, Set 1	1 - 4
ON5701	Cruella De Vil, the villainess, Set 2	1 - 4
ON5702	The Colonel and Sgt. Tibbs, the absent-	1 - 4

ON5710 ON5711 ON5712 ON5713

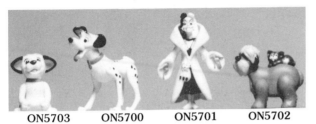

ON5703 ON5700 ON5701 ON5702

minded sheepdog and scruffy cat, Set 3

ON5703	Lucky, Dalmatian pup, Set 4	1 - 4
Boxes		
ON5710	Barn	1 - 3
ON5711	Dog's Leashes	1 - 3
ON5712	Piano	1 - 3
ON5713	Staircase	1 - 3
Point of Purchase		
ON5721	Translite, menu board	8 - 10
ON5722	Translite, drive-thru	6 - 8
ON5723	Counter Display w/premiums	60 - 90

ON5723

PE1100 PE1101 PE1102 PE1103 PE1105 PE1104

PE1120

PEANUTS, 1990

The popular Peanuts characters were placed in a farm setting for a national Happy Meal from Mar 30 to Apr 26, 1990. This year was the 40th anniversary of the Peanuts cartoon strip by Charles Schultz. Each of the main 4 premiums had 3 pieces and the two "Under 3" premiums were 1-piece figures. They were polybagged with the information printed on the bag.

Premiums		
PE1100	Snoopy's Hay Hauler – Snoopy, blue green hauler, yellow hay bale, Set 1	1 - 4
PE1101	Charlie Brown's Seed Bag 'n Tiller – Charlie Brown, yellow bag, blue & orange tiller, Set 2	1 - 4
PE1102	Lucy's Apple Cart – Lucy, green cart, red apple basket, Set 3	1 - 4
PE1103	Linus' Milk Mover – Linus, orange mover, gray milk can, Set 4	1 - 4
PE1104	Charlie Brown's Egg Basket (Under 3)	2 - 5
PE1105	Snoopy Potato Sack (Under 3)	2 - 5
Boxes		
PE1110	County Fair	1 - 3
PE1111	E–I–E–I–O!	1 - 3
PE1112	Field Day	1 - 3
PE1113	Hoe Down	1 - 3
Point of Purchase		
PE1120	Translite, menu board	6 - 10
PE1121	Translite, drive-thru	4 - 8
PE1122	Counter Display w/premiums	75 - 100

PE1110   PE1111   PE1112

PE1113

Back of 8010-13

PE8017

PETER RABBIT, 1988

The New England area gave children a chance to read some Beatrix Potter books during the fall of 1988. Besides the story, each book included reprints of the original water color illustrations also done by Beatrix Potter. The McDonald's logo appears on page 1 and on the back cover of these white 60-page 4" x 5" books.

Premiums

PE8010	*Tale of Benjamin Bunny*	7 - 14
PE8011	*Tale of Flopsy Bunnies*	7 - 14
PE8012	*Tale of Peter Rabbit*	7 - 14

PE1122

PE8020

PI1510　　　　　　　　　PI1511　　　　　　　　　PI1512

PE8010

PE8012

PE8011

PI1513

PE8013

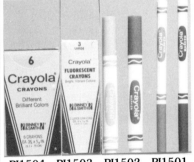

PI1504　PI1503　PI1502　PI1501

PI1504	6 Pack Crayons – black, blue, brown, green, red, yellow, $3^5/8$" x $5/16$"	5 - 6
Boxes		
PI1510	Birdie	2 - 4
PI1511	Fry Guys	2 - 4
PI1512	Grimace	2 - 4
PI1513	Ronald	2 - 4
Point of Purchase		
PI1520	Translite	8 - 12
PI1521	Message Center Insert, cardboard	6 - 10
PI1522	Permanent Display Header Card	4 - 6
PI1523	Menu Board Lug-On w/premiums	10 - 22

PE8013	*Tale of Squirrel Nutkin*	7 - 14
Boxes		
PE8017	Mr. McGregor's Garden	10 - 15
Point of Purchase		
PE8020	Translite, menu board	10 - 15
PE8021	Translite, drive-thru	8 - 12

PICTURE PERFECT, 1985

Crayola products made by Binney & Smith, Inc., Easton, PA were featured in a national option Happy Meal entitled "Picture Perfect." This promotion ran in some areas from Dec 28, 1984 to Jan 27, 1985 and in other areas beginning Jan 25, 1985. The front panel of each of the 4 boxes were printed with quick draw instructions for drawing a McDonaldland character.

Premiums

PI1501	Coloring Markers – blue or red, $5^5/8$"	2 - 3
PI1502	Drawing Markers – orange or green, 5"	2 - 3
PI1503	3 Pack Jumbo Fluorescent Crayons – ultra blue, ultra red, ultra yellow, 4" x $7/16$" "Promotional Pack"	5 - 6

PI1521

122

PI3515

PI3510

PI1901

PL7041

| PI3500 | PI3501 | PI3502 | PI3503 |

PL6002

PL7029

PL7035

PIGGSBURG PIGS, 1991

McDonald's tied in with another Saturday morning cartoon series in a regional Happy Meal, Mar 8 – Apr 12, 1991. Denver, CO; Columbus, OH and South Florida were among the areas which ran the promotion. Piggsburg Pigs is copyrighted by the Fox Children's Network, Inc. The promotion featured 4 characters and vehicles, plus 1 sack. All premiums came in a polybag with an insert card.

Premiums

PI3500	Portly & Pig Head on cycle w/side car, Set 1	3 - 5
PI3501	Piggy & Quackers on crate racer, Set 2	3 - 5
PI3502	Rembrandt in barnyard hot rod, Set 3	3 - 5

PI3503	Huff & Puff on catapult, Set 4	3 - 5
Sack		
PI3510	Eight Piggsburg Characters	1 - 4
Point of Purchase		
PI3515	Translite, menu board	8 - 12
PI3516	Translite, drive-thru	6 - 10

PIZZA HAPPY SACK, 1990

Selected stores began test marketing pizza in 1990 and 1991. A Pizza Happy Sack was developed for store use so kids could order a Pizza Happy Meal. Printing on the sack read "Caution: The toy in this bag may contain small parts and is not intended for children under 3. Ask about special toys for kids under 3." Whatever premium currently being offered in the regular Happy Meal was utilized for the Pizza Happy Meal. The sack measured 5" x 9^1/$_2$" and carried a 1989 copyright.

Sack

PI1901	Pizza Party, white w/color graphics	1 - 3

PLAY–DOH, 1983

A 4-week Play–Doh Happy Meal was run in the New England/Boston area in May of 1983. Play-Doh, a non-toxic modeling compound, was developed and introduced in Cincinnati, OH in 1955. Two-ounce cans of Play–Doh, made by Kenner Products, were the premiums. The Play-Doh containers were made of cardboard with a tin bottom. Four colors were offered. The box has not been identified.

Premiums

PL6001	Blue	5 - 10
PL6002	Red	5 - 10

PL6015

PL7040

PL6003	White	5 - 10
PL6004	Yellow	5 - 10
Point of Purchase		
PL6015	Translite, menu board	20 - 25

PLAY–DOH, 1984

The Wichita, KS and Nebraska markets ran the 1983 Play-Doh promotion in March of 1984. Due to company concerns, the cans of Play-Doh were not placed in the box with the food because of the type of ink used on the Play-Doh can. Nebraska ran the promotion from Mar 2 – April 1; while the Wichita area offered it Mar 23 – Apr 22. (See PL6001-04)

PLAY–DOH, 1985

Once again in 1985, Play-Doh was offered in Happy Meals. This time the promotion involved 6 colors and ran in KS, MS, TN, MO, IL, AR, OK (Feb 15 – Mar 29); MA, AL, TX (Mar 15 – May 26); northern IN (May 20 – June 30); and Nashville, TN and northern AL (Sept 13 – Oct 13). The Happy Meal box contained a proof-of-purchase coupon. For 3 proof-of-purchase coupons and $6.49 a Count Creepyhead and Friends playset could be obtained from the Play-Doh supplier.

Premiums
Blue (see PL6001)
Red (see PL6002)

PL7097

	White (see PL6003)	
	Yellow (see PL6004)	
PL7029	Pink	5 - 10
PL7030	Green	5 - 10
Box		
PL7035	Play-Doh Place	4 - 6
Point of Purchase		
PL7040	Translite, menu board/drive-thru (large)	10 - 15
PL7041	Table Tent	4 - 6
PL7042	Message Center Insert, cardboard	10 - 15

PLAY–DOH, 1986

A national Happy Meal with Play-Doh ran July 7 – Aug 3, 1986. Kenner developed a new container so all the 2-oz cans used in 1986 were made entirely of plastic. A total of 8 colors (2 per week) and 4 boxes were featured in this promotion.

Premiums

PL7075	Pink, Week 1	4 - 8
PL7076	Blue, Week 1	4 - 8
PL7077	Purple, Week 2	4 - 8
PL7078	Red, Week 2	4 - 8
PL7079	Green, Week 3	4 - 8
PL7080	Yellow, Week 3	4 - 8
PL7081	Orange, Week 4	4 - 8
PL7082	White, Week 4	4 - 8

PL7090   PL7091   PL7092   PL7093

Collect all 7 Playmobil people and figures.
You'll find one in every Happy Meal.

PL7920

PO7516

Boxes   PL7900–06

PL7090	Circus Animals	3 - 5
PL7091	Farm Animals	3 - 5
PL7092	House Pets	3 - 5
PL7093	Yesterday's Animals	3 - 5

Point of Purchase

PL7095	Translite, menu board/drive-thru (large)	10 - 12
PL7096	Translite, drive-thru (small)	8 - 10
PL7097	Message Center Insert, cardboard	10 - 12

PLAYMOBIL, 1981, Test

A Playmobil People Happy Meal was tested in Missouri (St. Louis, Columbia, Jefferson City, Springfield) and Nebraska from May 8 to June 25, 1981. Playmobil was developed by a West German company, Geobra-Brandstatter. Schapen Toys of Minneapolis, MN manufactured and introduced them in the U.S. in 1975. A Playmobil coupon was included with each of the 7 premium polybags. For 4 coupons and $1.25, a 5-piece Playmobil accessory set could be ordered. The set included a cannon, canoe and decal, tepee and decal, rocking chair and a road roller.

Premiums

PL7900	Indian (red) w/headpiece, shield, spear, rifle	- - 20
PL7901	Construction Worker (blue coat, dark blue trousers) w/ladder, hat, pick and shovel	- - 20
PL7902	Cavalry Soldier (blue jacket, light blue trousers, yellow hair) w/blue hat, rifle, flag w/a circle of stars and a #1 on it	- - 20
PL7903	Soldier's Horse (medium brown) w/long watering trough or oblong shaped watering trough	- - 20
PL7904	Umbrella Girl (blue dress, red arms/feet) w/ white hat, yellow umbrella	- - 20
PL7905	Farmer (green) w/white hat, white shovel, rake, scythe	- - 20

PL7906	Farmer's Cow (medium brown)	- - 20

Point of Purchase

PL7920	Tray Liner	8 - 10

PLAYMOBIL, 1982

Playmobil figures were to be featured in a national promotion Oct 22 – Nov 28, 1982. However, McDonald's cancelled the promotion into the second week and recalled those premiums already dispensed due to a safety concern of the many small accessory pieces. This incident prompted the design and offering of the special "Under 3" premiums for the Happy Meal.

Five figures with accessories were to have been offered. An 18-piece accessory set was available for 3 mail-in Happy Meal coupons and $1.99.

PL7950   PL7951   PL7952   PL7953   PL7954

Premiums

PL7950	Sheriff – black or yellow hair/black hat/ gray cape/brown rifle, Week 1	- - 10
PL7951	Indian – red or black hair/dark brown headdress/brown shield/spear and peace pipe (on plastic tree)/decal for shield/brown rifle, Week 2	- - 10
PL7952	Horse & Saddle – brown/long narrow brown water trough, Week 3	- - 15
PL7953	Umbrella Girl – red body w/white arms & feet/ yellow umbrella/ brown handle/yellow round bag/blue hat, Week 4	- - 15
PL7954	Farmer – green body/yellow hat/gray rake & scythe/brown dog, Week 5	- - 15

Boxes

PL7960	Barn	3 - 10
PL7961	Log Cabin	3 - 10

PL7961   PL7962   PL7960   PL7963

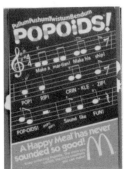

PO7516

PO7510

PO7511

PL7962	School House	3 - 12
PL7963	Trading Post	3 - 12
Point of Purchase		
PL7970	Translite, menu board/drive-thru (large)	10 - 15
PL7971	Recall Counter Card	10 - 15
PL7972	Crew Button	3 - 5

POPOIDS, 1984

Pullum, Pushum, Twistum, Bendum Popoids were the premiums in a St. Louis region Happy Meal from Mar 30 – May 6, 1984. There were 6 sets which came in a clear plastic bag, 6" x 8", with the Popoids name printed in red numerous times across the sack. No McDonald's identification appeared on the sack. Each bag included a Popoids cross-sell sheet showing sets which could be purchased in retail stores. One information sheet said there were 2 sets with ball joints; another sheet said

PL7970

PO7505

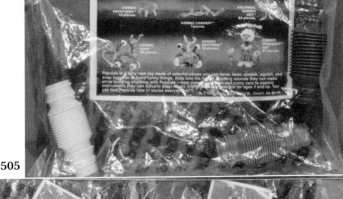

PO7500	PO7502

PO7503	PO7504

Dear Customer,

We have voluntarily stopped the distribution of the Playmobil toys because the Playmobil manufacturer failed to meet McDonald's specifications and governmental standards for children under the age of three.

The Playmobil toys contain pieces which, if broken, could be swallowed.

We recommend that the use of these Playmobil toys by children under the age of three be discontinued, and that these toys be returned to any McDonald's for a box of McDonald's cookies, a cone or a refund.

Thank you.

PL7971

PO7515

there were 2 sets with club joints. (See also: CRAZY CREA-TURES (Popoids), 1985)

Premiums

PO7500	#1, 2 bellows (blue, dark blue) & 1 white ball joint	– - 40	
PO7501	#2, 2 bellows & 1 ball joint (or maybe cube joint)	– - 40	
PO7502	#3, 2 bellows (blue, dark blue) & 1 white cube joint	– - 40	
PO7503	#4, 2 bellows (red, yellow) & 1 orange pentahedron joint	– - 40	
PO7504	#5, 2 bellows (red, yellow) & 1 orange column (wheel) joint	– - 40	
PO7505	#6, 3 bellows (blue, dark blue & yellow)	– - 40	

Boxes

PO7510	Elephoid – jungle scene	10 - 15
PO7511	Octopoid – undersea scene	10 - 15

Point of Purchase

PO7515	Translite, menu board/drive-thru (large)	20 - 25
PO7516	Table Tent	6 - 8
PO7517	Tray Liner	5 - 7

POTATO HEAD KIDS, 1987

Playskool Potato Head Kids were the premiums in a regional Happy meal, Feb 20 – Mar 19, 1987. Parts of TX, OK and NM ran the promotion. Each premium included a body, hat and shoes in a polybag printed with the age labeling. "Made in China. Safety tested for children of all ages. Recommended for ages 2 & up." The 12 Potato Head Kids premiums were not exclusive to McDonald's. Hasbro sold the same ones at retail. Some of the colors of the Kids' hats and shoes were different than what was printed on the box and large dangler. The actual colors given out are listed below. Playskool is a trademark owned by Hasbro, Inc.

Premiums

PO8000	Big Chip, red hat/blue shoes	– - 20
PO8001	Dimples, orange hat/pink shoes	– - 20
PO8002	Lolly, yellow hat/green shoes	– - 20
PO8003	Lumpy, green hat/yellow shoes	– - 20
PO8004	Potato Dumpling, blue hat/pink shoes	– - 20
PO8005	Potato 'Puff, pink hat/light purple shoes	– - 20
PO8006	Slick, purple hat/white shoes	– - 20
PO8007	Slugger, blue hat/yellow feet	– - 20
PO8008	Smarty Pants, yellow hat/purple shoes	– - 20
PO8009	Spike, blue hat/brown shoes	– - 20
PO8010	Spud, white hat/orange feet	– - 20

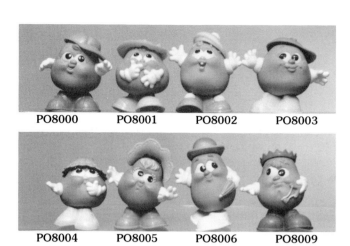

PO8000 PO8001 PO8002 PO8003

PO8004 PO8005 PO8006 PO8009

PO8010 PO8007 PO8008 PO8011

PO8015

PO8020

PO8022 (Potato Dumpling)

PO8022 (Spike)

PO8022 (Spud)

PO9015

PO9020

PO8021

PO8011	Tulip, purple hat/blue shoes	– - 20
Box		
PO8015	Potato Head Kids	8 - 12
Point of Purchase		
PO8020	Translite, menu board	10 - 15
PO8021	Large Dangler	10 - 15
PO8022	Register Topper, 1 premium in blister pack	10 - 20

PO9022 (Week 1)　　　PO9022 (Week 4)

PO9022 (Week 3)　　　PO9022 (Week 2)

POTATO HEAD KIDS, 1992

Playskool Potato Head Kids were again featured in a regional (OK, TX, parts of FL, AL, LA, eastern PA) Open Window in Feb 1992. The 8 premiums were similar to those used in the 1987 campaign, but changes were made in colors and facial features. Each premium came in a polybag with a red insert card which showed other Potato Head products available at retail stores. Two premiums were featured each week and could be placed on the register topper supplied to the stores.

Premiums

PO9001	Dimples, blue hat/purple feet, Week 1	– - 4
PO9002	Spike, light green hat/yellow feet, Week 1	– - 4
PO9003	Potato Dumpling, blue hat/pink feet, Week 2	– - 4
PO9004	Slugger, blue hat/yellow feet, Week 2	– - 4
PO9005	Slick, purple hat/white feet, Week 3	– - 4
PO9006	Tulip, purple hat/blue feet, Week 3	– - 4
PO9007	Potato Puff, pink hat/purple feet, Week 4	– - 4
PO9008	Spud, white hat/orange feet, Week 4	– - 4
Sack, 6" x 12"		
PO9015	Eight Potato Kids	1 - 2
Point of Purchase		
PO9020	Translite, menu board	8 - 12
PO9021	Translite, drive-thru	6 - 8
PO9022	Register Topper w/2 premiums ea, 4 different	6 - 8

PO9001　　PO9002　　PO9003　　PO9004

PO9005　　PO9006　　PO9007　　PO9008

RAGGEDY ANN & ANDY, 1989/90

This Happy Meal was a tie-in with the CBS Saturday morning TV show, "The Adventures of Raggedy Ann and Andy". The characters are not new as they became one of the first licensed properties 70 years ago. The 4 premiums, 1 "Under 3", and 1 box were tested in the Sept 1989 Open Window in the San Francisco region; Las Vegas; Portland, OR and Hawaii. It was later done in other areas in Sept 7 to Oct 4, 1990 Open Windows. The back of the insert card in each polybag carried a story about the character. The characters and playground equipment were created exclusively for McDonald's.

Premiums

RA3001	Raggedy Andy w/slide, yellow slide/red stand, Set 1	3 - 6
RA3002	Raggedy Ann w/swing, yellow swing/red stand, Set 2	3 - 6
RA3003	Grouchy Bear w/carousel, yellow carousel/red stand, Set 3	3 - 6
RA3004	Camel with the Wrinkled Knees w/seesaw, red seesaw/yellow stand, Set 4	3 - 6
RA3005	Camel with the Wrinkled Knees (Under 3) same as RA3004 w/o seesaw, but packaged w/insert card w/the "Under 3" black/white zebra stripes around the edge	- - 8

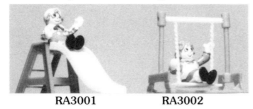

RA3001   RA3002

RA3003   RA3004   RA3005

Boxes

RA3010	School House	1 - 3

Point of Purchase

RA3020	Translite, menu board	10 - 12
RA3001	Translite, drive-thru	8 - 10

RAIN OR SHINE, 1989

Two generic Happy Meal boxes were produced in 1989. They were to be used during clean-up times or when the store ran out of themed boxes. There were no premiums produced to match the boxes.

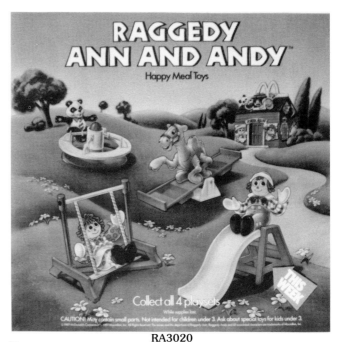

RA3020

Boxes

RA4000	Bubbles	1 - 3
RA4001	Umbrellas	1 - 3

READ ALONG WITH RONALD, 1989

Helping kids learn to read was the theme of a regional (New England area) Happy Meal in Sept 1989. Each of the 4 premiums, a cassette tape and book of the same color, came in a clear polybag. Children could read along in the book as they listened to the tape. Pictures in the book could also be colored. Each of the books carried a message of being a friend, sharing, helping others and believing in oneself. Two McDonaldland characters not featured very often in Happy Meals (Professor and Captain) were used in some of the stories. The books, 7" x 7", were 24 pages, plus cover. One bag was used.

Premiums

RE0500	*Dinosaur in McDonaldland*, green	5 - 15
RE0501	*Grimace Goes to School*, purple	5 - 15
RE0502	*The Day Birdie the Early Bird Learned to Fly*, yellow	5 - 15
RE0503	*The Mystery of the Missing French Fries*, red	5 - 15

Sack, 8½" x 11½"

RE0510	Ronald Reading, green & purple	4 - 6

Point of Purchase

RE0515	Translite, menu board	10 - 15
RE0516	Translite, drive-thru	8 - 12

RA3010   RA4000   RA4001

RE0501   RE0502   RE0500   RE0503

RE0510

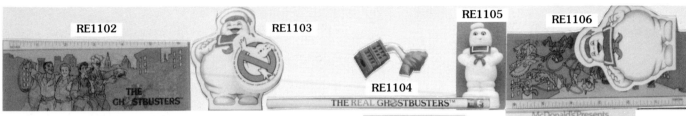

RE1102   RE1103   RE1105   RE1106

RE1104

REAL GHOSTBUSTERS, 1987

A back-to-school theme featuring Ghostbuster characters was the national option Happy Meal from Sept 4 – Oct 15, 1987. Kids know Ghostbusters from the 1984 movie and the Saturday morning TV cartoon show on ABC. All premiums were polybagged except for the pencil case and the ruler. Columbia Pictures holds the copyright for Ghostbusters.

Premiums

RE1101	Pencil Case, clear w/color graphics, $3^1/2$" x $8^1/4$", "The Real Ghostbusters Containment Chamber", Week 1	2 - 4
RE1102	X-O Graphic Ruler, 6", "The Real Ghostbusters", Week 2	2 - 4
RE1103	Notepad and Eraser, marshmallow on pad, Ghostbuster on eraser, Week 3	3 - 5
RE1104	Pencil and Pencil Topper, Green Slimer on topper, Week 4	4 - 6
RE1105	Pencil Sharpener, Ghost, white, Week 5	2 - 4
RE1106	Ruler & Notepad, same as RE1102 & notepad of RE1103 except packaged together for "Under 3"	4 - 6

Boxes

RE1110	Headquarters	1 - 3
RE1111	Museum	1 - 3
RE1112	Public Library	1 - 3
RE1113	Schoolhouse	1 - 3

Point of Purchase

RE1120	Translite, menu board	8 - 10
RE1121	Translite, drive-thru	6 - 8

RE1101

RE1163

REAL GHOSTBUSTERS, 1992

Bicycle accessories were featured for the Real Ghostbusters Happy Meal in the Kansas City area during the Open Window in Feb 1992. They had previously been offered in Canada, Mexico and Spain. The 4 premiums were designed to be mounted on the bike's handlebars and came with the hardware needed to do so. The P.K.E. Water Bottle was recalled the first of the promotion for reasons unknown and some stores did not release any of this item. Each premium came in a polybag with an insert card which had instructions for attaching the premium to the bike. One sack was used.

RE1110   RE1111   RE1112   RE1113

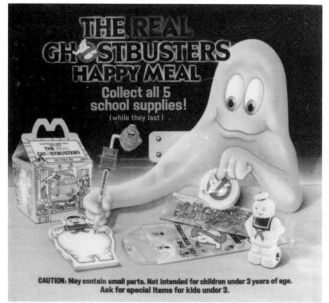

RE1120

RESCUERS DOWN UNDER, 1990

Walt Disney Pictures released *The Rescuers Down Under*, in November of 1990. This was a sequel to *The Rescuers* which was released in the spring of 1989. Australia is the location for *Rescuers Down Under* featuring the popular characters, Bernard and Bianca. The national Happy Meal, Nov 30 – Dec 27, 1990, provided 4 miniature translucent pocket viewers shaped like movie cameras. As the side handle was turned, a mini-movie appeared in the viewer. Four boxes came with the promotion, as did 1 premium for "Under 3". On the handle of each box was the logo of the International Literacy Year and the words "Share the Gift of Reading. Contact your local literacy program." All premiums were polybagged and were exclusive to McDonald's.

Premiums

RE6100	Bernard and Bianca, green camera w/yellow label, Week 1	1 - 3
RE6101	Jake, orange camera w/light green label, Week 2	1 - 3
RE6102	Cody, clear camera w/blue label, Week 3	1 - 3
RE6103	Wilbur, purple camera w/pink label, Week 4	1 - 3
RE6104	Bernard in a piece of cheese (1-pc rubber figure) (Under 3)	2 - 4

RE6100   RE6103   RE6102   RE6101   RE6104

Boxes

RE6110	Eagle	1 - 3
RE6111	Fireflies	1 - 3
RE6112	Lizard	1 - 3
RE6113	Rope	1 - 3

RE1150   RE1157   RE1153   RE1154   RE1158

Premiums

RE1150	Ecto Siren, white	2 - 4
RE1151	RE1150 w/separate sticker sheet	1 - 3
RE1152	Separate sticker sheet for RE1150	50¢ - 1
RE1153	Egon Spinner, green/yellow/blue	2 - 4
RE1154	P.K.E. Water Bottle, yellow/blue	- - 10
RE1155	RE1154 w/separate sticker sheet	2 - 4
RE1156	Separate sticker sheet for RE1154	50¢ - 1
RE1157	Slimer Horn, blue/green	2 - 4
RE1158	Slimer Squeezer, 1-pc green (Under 3)	2 - 5

Sack, 6" x 12"

RE1163	Real Ghostbusters	1 - 2

Point of Purchase

RE1165	Translite, menu board	8 - 12
RE1166	Translite, drive-thru	6 - 10

RESCUE RANGERS (See CHIP 'N DALE RESCUE RANGERS, 1989)

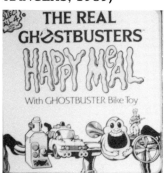

RE1165

RE6110   RE6111

RE6112   RE6113

131

RE6120

Point of Purchase

RE6120	Translite, menu board	8 - 10
RE6121	Translite, drive-thru	6 - 8

ROUND TOP, 1977, Test I

The St. Louis Regional Advertising Director, Dick Brams, asked 2 advertising agencies to develop ideas for a kid's meal. The Bernstein/Rein & Boasberg agency came up with the name "Happy Meal" which would include a hamburger or cheeseburger, fries, cookie sample, soft drink and a premium. The agency was based in Kansas City, MO, so the first test took place there as well as in several other cities where the ad agency handled accounts for McDonald's (Denver, CO; Wichita, KS; Phoenix, AZ; Tucson, AZ; Las Vegas, NV). The test ran from 11/4/77 to 2/5/78 in Kansas City and 11/4/77 to 12/2/77 in the other cities.

During this first test 3 round top boxes were produced. They were called "round tops" because the ends of the boxes were round and when put together the box had a rounded top "lunch box" appearance. Each 1977 copyrighted box was designed by a famous illustrator. Box #1 was illustrated by Simms Taback; #2 by Lionel Kalish; and #3 by Jack Geyer.

The first premiums produced for Happy Meals were 4

McDonaldland character x-o graph cards. A joke was printed on the back of each $1^1/_4$" x $1^1/_2$" card and the x-o graph copyright. The jokes were rotated among the cards so any one character card had a variety of jokes. These came in polybags.

Also in this test, soft plastic McWrist wallets were used. These were imprinted with the character's name and the McDonald's logo on the adjustable band. The featured character's face was molded on the lid of the coin holder. Imprinted on the bottom was "Pan Western Research Corp., Pat. Pend., Santa Anna, Calif."

McDonald character faces were imprinted in the top of the ring and then painted. These were of an "open back" design to fit all finger sizes. NOTE: The wrist wallets and rings were not produced just for the Happy Meal as they were already available from McDonald's supply companies.

Premiums

RO7001	X-O Graph Cards – Big Mac (7001), Captain (7002), Hamburglar (7003), Ronald (7004)	10 - 20
RO7005	McWrist Wallets – Big Mac (7005), Captain (7006), Hamburglar (7007), Ronald (7008); came in blue, green red, yellow (see color page 55)	2 - 4
RO7009	McDonaldland Rings – Big Mac (7009), yellow/blue; Captain (7010), orange/ black; Hamburglar (7011), yellow/black; Grimace (7012), purple/red; Ronald (7013), white/red	1 - 2

Boxes

RO7020	Riddle/What's Wrong Here?, Round Top #1	50 - 75
RO7021	Lion/Ronald/Big Mac, Round Top #2	50 - 75
RO7022	Giraffe/Ronald/Mayor/Big Mac/ Hamburglar, Round Top #3	50 - 75

Point of Purchase

RO7028	Translite, menu board	20 - 30
RO7029	Register Topper, $10^5/_8$" square	10 - 15
RO7030	Ceiling Dangler, food contents of Happy Meal	10 - 15

RO7030

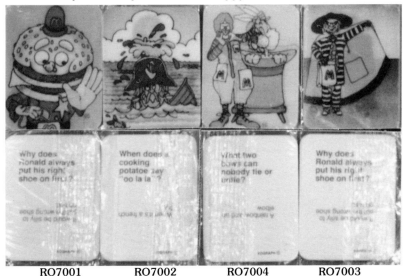

RO7001   RO7002   RO7004   RO7003

RO7021

RO7022   RO7020

RO7028

RO7029   RO7062-64

RO7010   RO7012   RO7011   RO7009   RO7013

RO7052   RO7053   RO7051   RO7054

RO7055

RO7065

ROUND TOP, 1978, Test II

The second test of the "Happy Meal" concept begin the day after Test I ended and ran until 6/30/78 in the Kansas City, MO area. Again, the boxes were designed by famous illustrators and the premiums used were available from McDonald's suppliers or other toy companies. Listed below are dates and premiums known to have been used.

Feb 6 – Mar 2: The McDonaldland Pencil Puppets were soft rubber character heads which fit over the tops of pencils. Later these were used in the CIRCUS WAGON, 1979 campaign.

Mar 3–17: an "Uncle O'Grimacy" character ring (Grimace with an Irish look) used this for the St. Patrick's Day time period. It had the same "open back" style as the rings used in Round Top Test I.

Mar 18 – Apr 8: McDonaldland Press-Ons were 3" round iron-ons patches, copyrighted 1978. They had a white background with color graphics of a McDonaldland character.

Apr 9–30: Three 3" x 4^1/$_2$" Ronald Magic Pads came in booklet form. When a pencil was rubbed over the pages, a character would appear. Book 1 featured Ronald, Mayor, Grimace; Book 2: Ronald, Big Mac, Captain Crook; and Book 3: Ronald, Hamburglar, Professor.

May 1–30: The Sundae Smile Saucer, copyright 1978, was a frisbee-type piece (5^3/$_4$" round) which had the name on the top half of the circle and a "smile" on the bottom half. McDonald's logos served as "cheeks". These were also used in a later test promotions (see GENERIC, 1979).

June 5 – July 3: The Space Raiders originally tested in the Fun-to-Go Happy Meal were offered during this time span.

A T-shirt and matching button was provided for the crew to wear to promote this test. The printing on the front of the shirt read: "McDonald's (tee hee) is tickled to bring you (chuckle) Happy Meals (ho ho ho)". Records indicate a kid's shirt and matching button could also be ordered as a local store option. This shirt read: "Happy Meal makes my tummy giggle (tee hee)" and carried the McDonald logo.

Premiums

RO7051	Pencil Puppets – Big Mac (7051), Captain (7052), Hamburglar (7053), Ronald (7054) – blue, green, pink, orange, yellow	2 - 4
RO7055	Uncle O'Grimacy Ring, green	1 - 3
RO7056	McDonaldland Press-Ons – Big Mac (7056), Captain (7057), Grimace (7058), Hamburglar (7059), Mayor (7060), Ronald (7061)	3 - 5
RO7062	Ronald Magic Pads,– Book 1 (7062), Book 2 (7063), Book 3 (7064)	1 - 3
RO7065	Sundae Smile Saucer – red, yellow Space Raiders (See FU7022)	2 - 4

Boxes

RO7080	Make-A-Face, Round Top #4	50 - 75
RO7081	Bee/Gas Pump/Elephant, Round Top #5	50 - 75
RO7082	Weird Space Creatures, Round Top #6	50 - 75

Point of Purchase

RO7085	Crew T-Shirt	10 - 20
RO7086	Crew Button	8 - 12
RO7087	Kid's T-Shirt	10 - 20
RO7088	Kid's button	8 - 12

RO7080

RO7081

RO7082

RO7056	RO7057	RO7058
RO7059	RO7060	RO7061

ROUND TOP, 1978, Test III

The next Happy Meal test and clean-up time ran from June 11 to Feb 2, 1979. Besides Kansas City, Buffalo, NY (7/31 – 9/19), Phoenix, AZ (mid-Sept thru Oct) and St. Louis (10/16 – 2/2/79) served as test areas.

Three new boxes were designed and once again, the premiums were from McDonald's supply companies' catalogs. Offering dates for known premiums are listed below.

One premium produced was made up of jokes turned in by children in the Kansas City area. Signs were put up in McDonald's stores which read, "We Buy Jokes. Make up a joke, maze, game or riddle. If your entry is judged as one of the best, we'll buy it with $5 worth of McDonald's Gift Certificates and publish your entry in one of the McDonald's Joke Books we're going to put in every Happy Meal this summer. Deadline: March 4, 1978. Enter Here." Each page had a child's joke, printed in the child's own handwriting, plus their name and city/state. The 4" x 5" joke books, featuring 32 jokes each, were given out in 1978 as follows: Book 1, July 17–23; Book 2, July 24–30; Book 3, July 31–Aug 6; Book 4, Aug 7–13.

Aug 14 – Sept 10: Miniature hard plastic spinning tops (later used in CIRCUS WAGON, 1979 and GENERIC, 1979) were offered and came with a circular paper insert printed with several McDonald Ms. This fit over the spindle of the top.

Sept 11 – Oct 8: Twelve-piece $3^1/2$" x $5^1/2$" jigsaw puzzles were designed for premium use. Each puzzle featured 2 McDonaldland characters involved in the painting of a portion of fence. When the 4 puzzles were placed side by side, a completed picture was formed

Sept 6–23: A variety of premiums were offered. Full color Rub-Offs of McDonald characters were produced. These $1^5/8$" x $2^3/8$" transfers could be applied to any clean flat surface by placing the rub-off over the area desired and rubbing over the sheet

with a coin. The Ring Around Ronald was a ring toss game. A pencil needed to be placed into a thin cardboard holder, thus becoming the post. Several rings were to be punched-out of the 4" x 12" piece to complete the ring toss game. Sun-refracting Bike Reflectors (copyrighted 1978) were also offered. These pressure-sensitive paper 1" x 3" retangular pieces offered a rainbow of colors in the sunlight.

Nov 24 – Dec 24: Five 5" x $7^1/2$" Color Your Own Christmas Ornaments were featured for the holiday season. These were thin cardboard punch-outs which could be colored and then assembled to become decorations. An *M* was printed on the one piece which was used as the hanger. A 1978 copyright date was printed on each one. Records have been found to indicate a Ronald McDonald Christmas stocking was also available during this time period. No other information is known about this.

Dec 25–31: This was a clean-up time. Stores were to use the ring toss game, rub-offs and bike reflectors mentioned above.

Jan 1 – Feb 2: Full color McDonaldland Comic Books were printed for use. These 8–page books measured $6^1/2$" x $3^1/2$"each and were copyrighted 1978.

Feb 3 – Test IV (See GENERIC (Happy Meal Test IV), 1979)

RO7100	RO7101	RO7102	RO7103

RO7110	RO7111	RO7112	RO7113

Premiums

RO7100	Joke Books – Book #1 (7100), red; Book #2 (7101), yellow; Book #3 (7102), green; Book #4 (7103), purple	15 - 25
RO7105	Tops – red, yellow, blue (?), green (?)	1 - 3
RO7110	Jigsaw Puzzles – Professor/Grimace (7110), Hamburglar/Mayor (7111), Captain/Big Mac (7112), Ronald/Fry Goblins (7113)	4 - 10
RO7114	McDonaldland Rub-Offs – Grimace (7114),	4 - 10

RO7140

RO7141

RO7142

RO7119-22

RO7116

RO7105

RO7169

RO7118

Captain (7115), Hamburglar (7116),
Ronald (7117)

RO7118	Ring Around Ronald, yellow	4 - 10
RO7119	Bike Reflectors, – Big Mac (7119), Captain (7120), Hamburglar (7121), Ronald (7122)	4 - 10
RO7130	Color Your Own Christmas Ornament: Gingerbread House, 5 pcs (7130); Reindeer, 6 pcs (7131); Rocking Horse, 5 pcs (7132); Snowflake, 6 pcs (7133); unknown (7134)	5 - 7
RO7135	Ronald Christmas Stocking	?
RO7140	Comic Book: *Ronald McDonald & the Fries Farmers*	4 - 10
RO7141	Comic Book: *Ronald McDonald Lends a Helping Hand*	4 - 10
RO7142	Comic Book: *Ronald McDonald in the Disappearing Act*	4 - 10

Boxes

RO7160	McDonaldland Adventure/Picture Puzzles, Round Top #7	50 - 75
RO7161	House/Six Windows, Round Top #8	50 - 75
RO7162	Hamburger Island, Round Top #9	50 - 75

Point of Purchase

RO7168	Translite, We Buy Jokes, menu board	20 - 30
RO7169	Counter Card, We Want Jokes	10 - 15

RO7168

RO7160

RO7162

RUNAWAY ROBOTS, 1987

Six spring-propelled molded plastic robot characters made up the premiums for Runaway Robots. This regional campaign ran in St. Louis (Feb 6–Mar 22, 1987) and in parts of NE, MI, ME, MA, TN, and northern AL. Runaway Robots are licensed by Sue L. Colburn, Milwaukee, WI. Each premium came poly-bagged with safety information on the bag. There was no McDonald's identification on the premium or the polybag.

Premiums

RU5000	Beak, blue	3 - 6

RU5002 RU5001 RU5003 RU5005 RU5000 RU5004

RO7161

RU5010

SA1015

SA1001 SA1002 SA1003 SA1004 SA1005 SA1006 SA1007 SA1008

RU5001	Bolt, purple	3 - 6
RU5002	Coil, green	3 - 6
RU5003	Flame, red	3 - 6
RU5004	Jab, yellow	3 - 6
RU5005	Skull, black	3 - 6
Box		
RU5010	Six Runaway Robots	1 - 4
Point of Purchase		
RU5015	Translite, menu board	10 - 12
RU5016	Translite, drive-thru	8 - 10
RU5017	Counter Mat	8 - 10

SAFARI ADVENTURE, 1980

For the Safari Adventure Happy Meal, June 2 – 29, 1980, the McDonald's Corporation developed 4 Happy Meal boxes and POP. The stores decided on their own premiums which

RU5017

RU5015

SA1016   SA1017   SA1018

SA1022

could be something from the McDonald's supply company catalogs or something each store, area, or region developed themselves. Some areas used animal figures made by the Diener Company. Each of the animals came in various colors: blue, brown, gray, orange, pink, purple and yellow. These are still available from Diener at the time of publication.

Suggested items from M-B Sales for this promotion included: Ronald & Grimace Combs, Grimace Sponge, Ronald Sponge, McDonaldland Pockets, Ronald & Grimace Fun Mold, McDonaldland Game Top, Hamburglar Foam Floater, McDonaldland Light Switch Cover, Ronald Whistle Ring, McDonaldland Pennants, Ronald Tip*N*Tilt, Hamburglar Hockey, Letterland Stationery, Fishin' Fun, Who's In the Zoo.

Premiums

SA1001	Alligator	50¢ - 1
SA1002	Ape	50¢ - 1
SA1003	Elephant	50¢ - 1
SA1004	Hippo	50¢ - 1
SA1005	Lion	50¢ - 1
SA1006	Monkey	50¢ - 1
SA1007	Rhino	50¢ - 1
SA1008	Tiger	50¢ - 1

Boxes		SA2720	
SA1015	Ronald/Grimace		10 - 20
SA1016	Ronald/Hyena		10 - 20
SA1017	Ronald/Monkey		10 - 20
SA1018	Ronald/Vines		10 - 20
Point of Purchase			
SA1020	Translite, menu board/drive-thru (large)		15 - 20
SA1021	Ceiling Dangler w/boxes		40 - 80
SA1022	Counter Card, dimensional		15 - 25

SAILORS, 1988

A national option Happy Meal, Jan 1 – 28, 1988 featured 4 floating toys to be played with inside during the winter weather. The 4 boats were in 2 or 3 pieces, attached to a plastic tree. Two "Under 3" premiums were also tub toys, but molded in 1-piece. Four boxes matched the theme of the toys. This promotion ran later in Canada, but the premiums were issued in different colors.

SA2701   SA2702   SA2703   SA2700

SA2705   SA2704

SA2710   SA2711   SA2712   SA2713

137

SA5611

SA5610

SA5602

SA5601   SA5600

WORKSHOP OF ACTIVITIES

SA5603

Premiums

SA2700	Grimace Sub, purple, 3 pcs, Week 1	3 - 7
SA2701	Fry Kids Ferry, green, 3 pcs, Week 2	3 - 7
SA2702	Hamburglar Pirate Ship, blue, 3 pcs, Week 3	3 - 7
SA2703	Ronald Airboat, red, 4 pcs, Week 4	3 - 7
SA2704	Grimace Speedboat (Under 3)	3 - 5
SA2705	Fry Guy Floater (Under 3)	3 - 5

Boxes

SA2710	Fry Guy Afloat	2 - 4
SA2711	Houseboats	2 - 4
SA2712	Island Eyes	2 - 4
SA2713	Ronald Fishing	2 - 4

Point of Purchase

SA2720	Translite, menu board	10 - 12
SA2721	Translite, drive-thru	8 - 10

SAND CASTLE (see CASTLEMAKER, 1987)

SANTA CLAUS THE MOVIE, 1985

The Christmas promotion for 1985 (Nov 22 – Dec 24) featured books based on the Tri-Star Pictures release, *Santa Claus The Movie*. The picture was directed by the Salkinds and Pierre Spengler and Henry Mancini wrote the musical score. "Patch", Santa's elf assistant, played by Dudley Moore, was one of the main characters. The 2 storybooks (8" x 8", 24 pages) contained full-color photos from the movie. The 2 activity/coloring books (8" x

10¹/₂", 16 pages) included games, puzzles, connect-the-dots and scenes to color from the movies. Each of the 2 boxes had 3 panels which could be cut out and interlocked to make the Elves' Village. The other panel had cut-out figures from the story.

Premiums

SA5600	*The Elves at the Top of the World*, green storybook	2 - 4
SA5601	*The Legend of Santa Claus*, red storybook	2 - 4
SA5602	*Sleighful of Surprises*, green activity/coloring book	3 - 5
SA5603	*Workshop of Activities*, red activity/coloring book	3 - 5

Boxes

SA5610	Cottage	4 - 6
SA5611	Workshop	4 - 6

Point of Purchase

SA5615	Translite, menu board/drive-thru (large)	10 - 12
SA5616	Translite, drive-thru (small)	8 - 10

SA5617

SA5615

SC3420   SC3421   SC3422

| SA5617 | Counter Card | 6 - 8 |
| SA5618 | Tray Liner | 3 - 5 |

SCHOOL DAYS, 1984

Back to school items were in the School Days Happy Meal from Aug 20 to Oct 25, 1984. With 3 pencils, 5 erasers, 1 ruler, 1 pencil case and 2 pencil sharpeners, a total of 12 premiums were provided. The 4 boxes each featured a major school subject.

Premiums

SC3400	Eraser, white, dated 1984 – Birdie (3400), Captain (3401), Grimace (3402), Hamburglar (3403), Ronald (3404)	2 - 4
SC3405	Pencil, white, 7" w/eraser – Grimace (3405), Hamburglar (3406), Ronald (3407)	2 - 4
SC3408	Pencil Case, clear plastic, dated 1984, snap closure	1 - 3
SC3409	Grimace Pencil Sharpener, polybag	2 - 5
SC3410	Ronald Pencil Sharpener, polybag	2 - 5
SC3411	Ruler, 6", dated 1984	1 - 3

Boxes

SC3420	1, 2, 3	2 - 4
SC3421	ABC's	2 - 4
SC3422	History	2 - 4
SC3423	Science	2 - 4

Point of Purchase

SC3430	Translite, menu board/drive-thru (large)	10 - 12
SC3431	Message Center Insert, cardboard	10 - 12

SC3430

SC3405-07   SC3411

SC3400-10

SC3408

SC3423

SC3434

SE0205

SC3432	Permanent Display Header Card	4 - 6
SC3433	Menu Board Lug-On	4 - 6
SC3434	Food Item Lug-On	2 - 4

SEA WORLD OF OHIO, 1988

Sea World of Ohio is located a few miles southeast of Cleveland. A special Happy Meal ran in this area during the spring of 1988. The 3 painted hard rubber sea animal premiums were similar to those sold at Sea World, but the ones from McDonald's had the wording "Made in China, 1987, Sea World, Inc." on the bottom of each piece rather than on the sides of the figures. They came in a polybag with safety information printed on the bag.

Premiums
SE0200	Dolly Dolphin, gray/light blue, 3"	5 - 15
SE0201	Perry Penguin, black/white/orange, 3"	5 - 15
SE0202	Shamu Whale, white/black, 3"	5 - 15

Box
| SE0205 | Whale/3 Kids | 4 - 6 |

Point of Purchase
| SE0210 | Translite, menu board | 10 - 15 |
| SE0211 | Translite, drive-thru | 8 - 12 |

SEA WORLD OF TEXAS, 1988

Sea World of Texas, located in San Antonio, and McDonald's teamed up for a regional Happy meal which ran in 1988. Four 6" stuffed sea animals were offered in polybags;

each premium had a Sea World tag with safety information printed on it.

Premiums
SE0800	Dolphin, gray/white w/black eyes	3 - 8
SE0801	Penguin, black/white w/orange beak & feet	3 - 8
SE0802	Walrus, brown w/white face & tusks	3 - 8
SE0803	Whale, black/white	3 - 8

Box
| SE0810 | Ronald in Yellow Sub, copyright 1988 | 10 - 15 |

Point of Purchase
SE0815	Translite, menu board	15 - 20
SE0816	Translite, drive-thru	10 - 15
SE0817	Counter Display Card w/premiums, 21½" square, 1988 copyright	70 - 90

SEA WORLD OF TEXAS, 1989

A second Sea World of Texas Happy Meal ran in the Texas area during the summer of 1989. Of the 5 premiums used, 2

SE0200   SE0201   SE0202

SE0800   SE0801   SE0803   SE0802

SE0211

SE0815

SE0817

SE0810 - front   SE0810 - back   SE0830 - back

SE0800   SE0803   SE0825

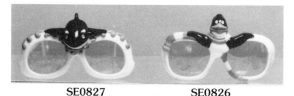

SE0827   SE0826

were the same as used in 1988. All 3 stuffed animals were polybagged and the sunglasses were double bagged. The box design was the same as used in 1988 except that a $2.50 cutout discount couple for Sea World was printed on the back.

Premiums
Dolphin (See SE0800)
Whale (See SE0803)

SE0837

SE0835

SE0825	Sea Otter, brown	2 - 6
SE0826	Penguin Sunglasses, white	2 - 6
SE0827	Whale Sunglasses, white/black/blue	2 - 6
Box		
SE0830	Ronald in Yellow Sub, copyright 1989, coupon on back	10 - 15
Point of Purchase		
SE0835	Translite, menu board	15 - 20
SE0836	Translite, drive-thru	10 - 15
SE0837	Counter Display Card w/premiums, 21½" square, 1989 copyright	70 - 90

SHIP SHAPE, 1983

Four vacuform boats which could float were the premiums for a national Happy meal offered June 6 – July 18, 1983. The food was placed inside the boat and the top and bottom then locked together. Each boat came with a decal sticker sheet as well as instructions on how to attach a string to make the boat into a pull toy. The boat bottom piece and the decal sheet carry a 1983 copyright date. Prices listed for SH5001-04 assume the stickers are applied.

Premiums
SH5001	Hamburglar Jet Boat, "The Splash Dasher", white top/orange bottom, Week 1	5 - 8
SH5002	Grimace Tug Boat, "Tubby Tugger",	5 - 8

	pink top/blue bottom, Week 2	
SH5003	Captain Crook Submarine, "Rub-a-Dub Sub", green top & bottom, Week 3	5 - 8
SH5004	Ronald McDonald Riverboat, "The Riverboat", yellow top/red bottom, Week 4	5 - 8
SH5005	SH5001-04 boat only	4 - 6
SH5006	SH5001-04 boat & separate sticker sheet	8 - 12
SH5007	SH5001-04 sticker sheet only	3 - 5

Point of Purchase

SH5015	Translite, 1983 copyright, menu board/drive-thru (large)	10 - 15
SH5016	Message Center Insert, 1983 copyright	10 - 15
SH5017	Counter Display w/1 premium per week 1983 copyright, motion	70 - 90

SH5002 SH5003 SH5004

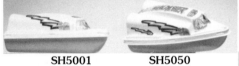

SH5001 SH5050

SH5015

SH5007

SH5055

SH5054

SH5017

SHIP SHAPE, 1985

"Ship Shape" ran twice on a national basis. The second time was May 31 – June 30, 1985. The four boats were the same as

used in 1983 except the sticker sheet for the Hamburglar Jet Boat, "The Splash Dasher", was redesigned. The small "Splash Dasher" name sticker was changed to a large "Splash Dasher" sticker which ran down the length of the top of the boat. The boat bottoms still carried a 1983 copyright, but all sticker sheets were newly printed and carried a 1985 copyright. Two tub toys were used for "Under 3" offerings.

Premiums

SH5050	Same as SH5001 w/1985 stickers Same as SH5002 Same as SH5003 Same as SH5004	5 - 8
SH5051	SA5001-4, boat & separate 1985 sticker sheet	8 - 12
SH5052	1985 Sticker sheet only	3 - 5
SH5054	Grimace Tub Toy, purple (Under 3)	1 - 5
SH5055	Fry Guy & Friend Tub Toy (Under 3)	1 - 5

Point of Purchase

SH5060	Translite, 1985 copyright, menu board/drive-thru (large)	10 - 12
SH5061	Translite, drive-thru (small)	6 - 8
SH5062	Message Center Insert, 1985 copyright	10 - 12
SH5063	Counter Display w/1 premium per week, 1985 copyright, motion	70 - 90
SH5064	Menu Board Lug-On w/3 premiums	18 - 24

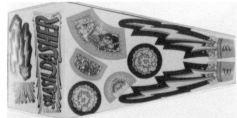

SH5052

SKY–BUSTERS, 1982

Matchbox Sky-Buster airplanes were selected by some regions as their choice for premiums sometime during 1982. The 6 different planes came in soft or hard rubber and in a variety of colors: purple, blue, pink, yellow, brown, orange, light green and dark green. Each plane had the name imprinted on it plus the Matchbox and Lesney names on the bottom. Matchbox is the registered trademark of Lesney Products, London, England. Soft planes are worth 50¢ - $1.

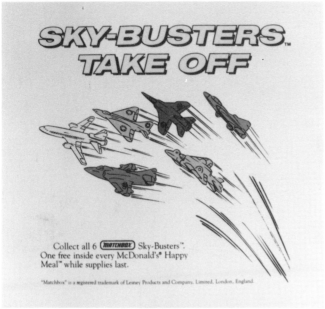

SK8015

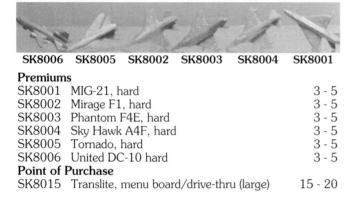

SK8006 SK8005 SK8002 SK8003 SK8004 SK8001

Premiums

SK8001	MIG-21, hard	3 - 5
SK8002	Mirage F1, hard	3 - 5
SK8003	Phantom F4E, hard	3 - 5
SK8004	Sky Hawk A4F, hard	3 - 5
SK8005	Tornado, hard	3 - 5
SK8006	United DC-10 hard	3 - 5

Point of Purchase

SK8015	Translite, menu board/drive-thru (large)	15 - 20

SPACE, 1979

McDonald's Corporation developed 6 boxes simply entitled "Happy Meal" for use nationally. These featured space scenes and were offered during the fall of 1979. Each area selected the premiums to be included. Starting Aug 16, 1979 the St. Louis/KC area elected to use Space Aliens, which were also called Alien Creatures. These were issued in blue, brown, pink, orange, yellow and various shades of green. Other areas used Space Raiders (see FUN–TO–GO).

Premiums

SP0090	Gill Face Creature	50¢ - 1
SP0091	Horned Cyclops	50¢ - 1
SP0092	Insect Man	50¢ - 1

SP0092   SP0093   SP0094   SP0097   SP0096   SP0095   SP0091   SP0090

SP0110

SP0111

SP0100   SP0101   SP0102

SP0103   SP0104   SP0105

SP0113

SP0150

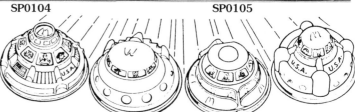

SP0200   SP0201   SP0202   SP0203

Out of this world.
Unidentified Happy Meal™

collect them all

SP0210

SP0093	Lizard Man	50¢ - 1
SP0094	Tree Trunk Monster	50¢ - 1
SP0095	Vampire Bat Creature	50¢ - 1
SP0096	Veined Cranium Creature	50¢ - 1
SP0097	Winged Amphibian Creature	50¢ - 1
Boxes		
SP0100	Big Mac/6 Martians	15 - 25
SP0101	Grimace/Shakes	15 - 25
SP0102	Space Creature	15 - 25
SP0103	Plant-a-tarium	15 - 25
SP0104	Ronald/Stowaways	15 - 25
SP0105	Space Zoo	15 - 25
Point of Purchase		
SP0110	Translite, Space Aliens, menu board	15 - 25
SP0111	Translite, Alien Creatures, menu board	15 - 25
SP0112	Translite, Happy Meal, menu board	15 - 25
SP0113	Counter Card	10 - 15
SP0114	Ceiling Dangler w/boxes	90 - 125

SPACE THEME, 1991

A generic Happy Meal sack with Ronald in a spaceship appeared in 1991. The 6" x 11" sack was white with color graphics and used in clean-up times or when a store ran out of the scheduled Happy Meal boxes or sacks.

Sack

SP0150	Ronald in Spaceship	1 - 3

SPACESHIP (Unidentified Happy Meal), 1981, Test

The test for the Spaceship Happy Meal ran in the Kansas City area in 1981. This promotion's official name was "Unidentified Happy Meal". Each of the 4 vacuform ships consisted of 3 parts: top, bottom and a sticker sheet. The top and bottom were secured together by snapping the bottom under the 4 tab locks in the top. The sticker sheet had decals featuring the McDonald's characters and on the back, "Exclusive at McDonald's! Unidentified Happy Meal" with instructions and copyright information. The color of each ship and whether each ship came in more than one color has yet to be confirmed. Ship styles 1, 2, and 4 are shown on color page 112.

Premiums

SP0200	Spaceship 1, 8 windows, stickers applied	10 - 20
SP0201	Spaceship 2, rounded front	10 - 20
SP0202	Spaceship 3, pointed front	10 - 20
SP0203	Spaceship 4, 4 knobs	10 - 20
SP0204	SP0200-03, spaceship only	4 - 8
SP0205	SP0200-03, spaceship & separate sticker sheet	15 - 25
SP0206	SP0200-03, sticker sheet only	8 - 10
Point of Purchase		
SP0210	Translite	20 - 30

SPACESHIP, 1982

The national Spaceship Happy Meal ran from Jan 22 – Feb

144

28, 1982. There were 4 ships in 4 colors each for a total of 16 offerings. There were 2 sets of sticker sheets. One set came with the ship pictured on the decal side of the sheet; the other did not. Also the Ronald character decal was slightly different between the 2 sets. Some ships have been found with a 8 tab lock system or a circle lock system to connect the top and bottom together. Some variance in the shades of colors (blue, green, red, yellow) have shown up and some #2 and #4 ships have a molded circle around the *M* on the top.

Premiums

SP0230	Spaceship 1, 8 windows	10 - 16
SP0231	Spaceship 2, rounded front	10 - 16
SP0232	Spaceship 3, pointed front	10 - 16
SP0233	Spaceship 4, 4 knobs	10 - 16
SP0234	SP0230-33 spaceship only	5 - 7
SP0235	SP0230-33 spaceship & separate sticker sheet	15 - 20
SP0236	Sticker Sheet only	3 - 5

Point of Purchase

SP0240	Translite	15 - 20
SP0241	Ceiling Dangler	25 - 40
SP0242	Counter Card, 1 ship featured each week	30 - 50

SP0206 (back)

SP0242

SPACESHIP (Glo–Trons), 1986

Spaceships were featured once again as a regional Happy Meal in 1986. This time the 4 ship designs had a silver-speckled metallic look. Each ship came only in 1 color and darker shades of blue, green and red were used along with a new gray color. The "Glo–Tron" name was derived from the stickers which glowed in the dark. The McDonald's name, 1985, and "Safety tested for children of all ages. Recommended for children Age 1 and over" were molded into the bottom of each ship.

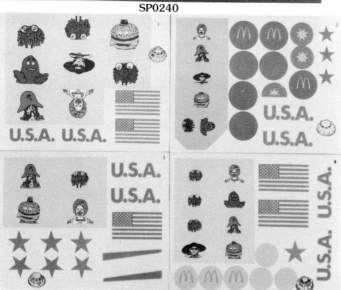

SP0240

SP0236 (front)

SP0315

SP7010

SP7011

SP7042

SP0236 - *back*

SP0307 - *back*

Premiums

SP0301	Spaceship 1, 8 windows, gray	10 - 20
SP0302	Spaceship 2, rounded front, blue	10 - 20
SP0303	Spaceship 3, pointed front, green	10 - 20
SP0304	Spaceship 4, 4 knobs, red	10 - 20
SP0305	SP0301-04, spaceship only	8 - 10
SP0306	SP0301-04, spaceship & separate sticker sheet	15 - 25
SP0307	SP0301-04, sticker sheet only	10 - 15

Point of Purchase

SP0315	Translite, menu board	15 - 25

SP7003	SP7004	SP7001	SP7002

SPORT BALL, 1988

Twenty plus stores in the Springfield, MO area test marketed the Sport Ball Happy Meal in Jul–Aug, 1988. All premiums were produced by Simon Marketing and came in polybags with an insert card.

Premiums

SP7001	Football, soft vinyl, yellow top half/red bottom half, Ronald McDonald's name in script on both sides, $3^1/2$" x $2^1/4$"	10 - 15
SP7002	Tennis Ball, soft sponge material, yellow, *M* engraved into ball, $2^1/2$" round	10 - 15
SP7003	Baseball, hard plastic, white, *M* molded onto ball, 3" round	10 - 15
SP7004	Basketball, soft sponge material, orange, 2" round, orange hoop w/white net w/suction cup for hanging. No McDonald identification on any basketball item.	10 - 15
SP7005	Same as SP7003, but w/"Under 3" card (black & white stripes on edge of polybag)	– - 15

Boxes

SP7010	Clear the Court	8 - 12
SP7011	Match Point	8 - 12

SP7017

SP7035

CAUTION: Basketball and hoop may contain small parts. Not intended for children under 3. Ask about special toys for kids under 3.

SP7015

Have a ball.

THE **SPORTSBALL** HAPPY MEAL

Get a different sportsball each week. Collect all four.

SP7016

Point of Purchase

SP7015	Translite, menu board	15 - 20
SP7016	Translite, drive-thru	10 - 15
SP7017	Counter Display w/premiums, motion	150 - 175

SPORTS BALL, 1990

Four soft vinyl sports balls were offered during an Open Window time from Sept 7 to Oct 4, 1990. Some regions offered them in Mar 1991. All were produced by M-B Sales. Each came in a polybag with an insert card which read "Collect all Four! - While Supplies Last."

Premiums

SP7025	Baseball, white w/red stitching & red McDonald's logo, 2¹/₄" round	2 - 4
SP7026	Basketball, orange w/black seams & black/white McDonald's logo, 2¹/₄" round	2 - 4
SP7027	Football, yellow w/red lacing & red/white	2 - 4

SP7025	SP7026	SP7027	SP7028

	McDonald's logo, 3¹/₄" long		
SP7028	Soccer Ball, red & yellow w/yellow/white McDonald's logo	2 - 4

Box

SP7035	Ronald at Bat	1 - 3

Point of Purchase

SP7040	Translite, menu board	8 - 10
SP7041	Translite, drive-thru	6 - 8
SP7042	Counter Card w/premiums	10 - 20

SP7056	SP7055	SP7057	SP7058

SPORTS BALL, 1991

In Aug 1991, a variation of the 1990 Sports Ball Happy Meal came out during the clean-up time following the Barbie/Hot Wheels promotion. Basically, the 4 soft vinyl balls were the same as the 1990 ones, but with slightly different color shades. However, the football was brown with yellow laces and a yellow M. The other major difference was the information on the identification tag. In 1990, the white tag read, "M-B Sales, Oak Brook, IL" plus the material listing and location of manufacture. The 1991 tag did not include the "Oak Brook, IL" notation. Both tags carried a 1989 date. These came in a polybag with an insert card which did not have any "Collect all 4! – While Supplies Last" notation. Since this was a clean-up period offering, no special box or POP were created.

Premiums

SP7055	Baseball, white w/red stitching & red McDonald's logo, 2¹/₄" round	4 - 6
SP7056	Basketball, orange w/black seams & black/white McDonald's logo, 2¹/₄" round	4 - 6
SP7057	Football, brown w/yellow lacing & yellow M logo, 3¹/₄" long	4 - 6
SP7058	Soccer Ball, red & yellow w/yellow/white McDonald's logo	4 - 6

STAR TREK, 1979/80

The third national Happy Meal was a tie-in with the hit movie from Paramount Pictures, *Star Trek: The Motion Picture*. This was the first national Happy Meal with premiums designed to fit the theme. It ran Dec 26, 1979 to Feb 3, 1980 under the office name of "Star Trek Meal". The word *Happy* was not used on the boxes or advertising pieces.

The plastic Communicator was issued in 2 colors, black or silver, and resembled a walkie talkie with a moving antenna. Each communicator came with operation instructions printed on the bag. A mini 8-frame movie was included with each communicator and could be viewed by turning the side crank. Each movie strip contained 2 comics, one on each side. There were 5 different comics. The 2 comics printed back to back were not always the same combination.

Each of the 4 Hidden Compartment Space Rings came in blue, red or yellow and featured a different Star Trek character or design engraved on the top: Captain Kirk, *U.S.S. Enterprise*, Mr. Spock or the Star Trek logo. The hidden compartment was revealed when the top of the ring was lifted.

Four iron-on transfers included a character transfer (featuring Capt. Kirk, Dr. McCoy, Lt. Ilia, Mr. Spock) and an official Star

147

ST2020　　　　ST2021　　　　ST2022

Trek logo transfer. Lt. Ilia came with a green or yellow color band printed around the character.

The blue plastic Navigation Wrist Bracelet came with a set of 6 color decals to be used to decorate the bracelet. A navigation chart which could be placed under a special panel on the bracelet to view scenes of the galaxy was included.

The Star Trek Starfleet Game was designed to be played by 4 players. Playing pieces and rolling die were punch-outs from the end of the colored cardboard game. Each player tried to be the first to move his ship to V'Ger.

Polybags were used to enclose the communicator, iron-on transfers and wrist bracelet.

The translite featuring food items had a motorized pin wheel unit behind it which caused the stars to twinkle.

ST2001

ST2006　　ST2007　　ST2008　　ST2009

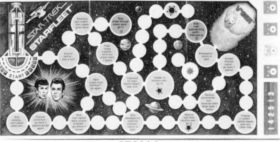

ST2016

ST2012　　ST2011　　ST2010　　ST2013

Premiums

ST2001	Communicator w/comic strip #1, *Star Trek Stars*	8 - 15
ST2002	Communicator w/comic strip #2, *A Pill Swallows the Enterprise*	8 - 15
ST2003	Communicator w/comic strip #3, *Time and Time and Time Again*	8 - 15
ST2004	Communicator w/comic strip #4, *Votec's Freedom*	8 - 15
ST2005	Communicator w/comic strip #5, *Starlight, Starfight*	8 - 15
ST2006	Ring – Captain Kirk	8 - 12
ST2007	Ring – *U.S.S. Enterprise*	8 - 12
ST2008	Ring – Mr. Spock	8 - 12
ST2009	Ring – Star Trek logo	8 - 12
ST2010	Iron-On Transfer – Captain Kirk	8 - 15
ST2011	Iron-On Transfer – Dr. McCoy	8 - 15
ST2012	Iron-On Transfer – Lt. Ilia	8 - 15
ST2013	Iron-On Transfer – Mr. Spock	8 - 15

ST2023　　　　ST2024　　　　ST2025

ST2030

ST2031

ST2033

ST2015

ST2034

ST2032	Ceiling Dangler, displaying 5 boxes (see front cover)	70 - 140
ST2033	Counter Card, dimensional	15 - 30
ST2034	Crew Badge, paper	5 - 10

STENCILS & CRAYONS, 1991

Two plastic stencils, identical to ones used in the national 1987 Crayola Happy Meal, were used as clean-up premiums following the Barbie/Hot Wheels promotion in Aug 1991 and again at the end of Jan 1992. Each came in a polybag with a box of 4 crayons (blue, green, red and yellow) and the identification card. Crayon boxes were either yellow and white or red and blue. Both boxes carried a Prang Color Art label.

Premiums

| ST3101 | Grimace Stencil, purple, w/crayons | 1 - 3 |
| ST3102 | Ronald Stencil, red, w/crayons | 1 - 3 |

STICKER CLUB, 1985

Kids love stickers of all kinds, so a 10-week national Happy

ST3101   ST3102

ST2015	Navigation Wrist Bracelet, 8³/₄"	8 - 12
ST2016	Starfleet Game, 10¹/₄" x 5"	6 - 10
Boxes		
ST2020	Bridge/Draw the Alien	10 - 20
ST2021	Bridge/Planet Faces	10 - 20
ST2022	Federation	10 - 20
ST2023	Klingons	10 - 20
ST2024	Spacesuit	10 - 20
ST2025	Transporter	10 - 20
Point of Purchase		
ST2030	Translite, featuring a box, menu board/ drive-thru (large)	25 - 40
ST2031	Translite, featuring food items w/motion pinwheel for twinkle effect	30 - 45

ST4010   ST4011   ST4012   ST4013

Meal provided 5 sets of stickers featuring McDonaldland characters during the Mar 11 to May 19, 1985 time period. The recommendation was made to the stores to offer a different sticker sheet each day. The order was: paper, scented, motion, shiny, puffy. This sequence was repeated 14 times during the 70 days, thus each sticker sheet was offered once every 5 days. All sets were overwrapped with cellophane and some stickers had a tie-in with the box graphics.

Premiums

ST4001	Paper, 4-color, 12 stickers, $3^1/_2$" x 10" folded to $3^1/_2$" x 5"	4 - 7
ST4002	Scented, 4-color, 5 stickers, $3^1/_2$" x 5"	4 - 7
ST4003	Motion, X-O graphic, 4 stickers $2^1/_2$" x $2^1/_2$"	4 - 7
ST4004	Shiny, prismatic diffraction, 6 stickers, 3" x 4"	4 - 7
ST4005	Puffy, 2 stickers, $2^3/_4$" x $4^1/_2$"	4 - 7

ST4002   ST4004   ST4005

ST4001   ST4003   ST5509

Boxes

ST4010	Club House Meeting	2 - 4
ST4011	Sticker Club Party	2 - 4
ST4012	Sticker Club Picnic	2 - 4
ST4013	Trading Days	2 - 4

Point of Purchase

ST4020	Translite	10 - 12
ST4021	Message Center Insert	10 - 12
ST4022	Permanent Display Header Card	8 - 10
ST4023	Menu Board Lug-On w/premiums	15 - 25

STOMPER MINI 4x4, Push–Along, 1985

Schaper Manufacturing produced special non-motorized vehicles, "Stomper Mini 4x4 Push–Alongs", for a 6-week promotion from Sept 6 to Oct 17, 1985 in the St. Louis and Memphis areas. Stompers which are sold in retail stores are battery-powered. The 6 Push–Along premiums featured inde-

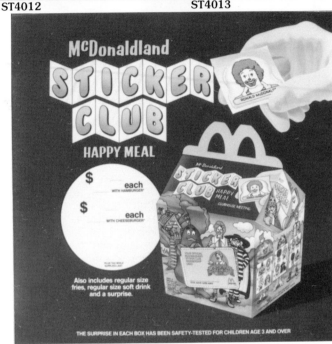

ST4020

pendent suspensions, white plastic wheels and black rubber tires. Two vehicles were modified – wheel and tire constructed as a single piece of black plastic – to be acceptable as "Under 3" premiums. Each polybag contained a proof-of-purchase coupon to be used in a mail-in offer for a limited edition battery-operated McDonald's Stomper 4x4. This special 4x4 had 3 speeds, working headlights and was available for 3 proof-of-purchase seals plus $1.99.

ST5502   ST5501   ST5503   ST5506

ST5505   ST5504   ST5507   ST5508

Premiums

ST5501	Chevy S-10, black	2 - 10
ST5502	Chevy S-10, yellow	2 - 10
ST5503	Chevy Van, red	2 - 10
ST5504	Dodge Rampage, white	2 - 10
ST5505	Dodge Rampage, blue	2 - 10
ST5506	Jeep Renegade, maroon	2 - 10
ST5507	Chevy Van, yellow (Under 3)	4 - 15
ST5508	Jeep Renegade, orange (Under 3)	4 - 15

ST5515

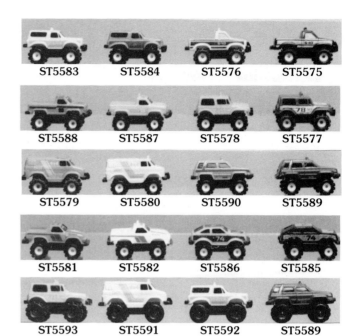

ST5583	ST5584	ST5576	ST5575
ST5588	ST5587	ST5578	ST5577
ST5579	ST5580	ST5590	ST5589
ST5581	ST5582	ST5586	ST5585
ST5593	ST5591	ST5592	ST5589

ST5509	Limited Edition McDonald's Stomper, battery-operated	5 - 10

Box

ST5515	Stompers in Desert	10 - 12

Point of Purchase

ST5520	Translite, menu board/drive-thru (large)	10 - 15
ST5521	Translite, drive-thru (small)	8 - 12
ST5522	Table Tent	4 - 6

STOMPER MINI 4x4, 1986

For the national Mini Stomper Happy Meal, Aug 8 – Sept 7, 1986, the number of premiums increased to 16. Eight different Stomper cars came in 2 colors. The clear polybag had the following printed in blue letters, "Stomper Mini 4x4. Safety tested for children age 3 and over. Caution: May contain small parts and is not intended for children under 3." Inside each bag was a Stomper booklet which included a proof-of-purchase. The same limited edition battery-operated McDonald's Stomper as offered in 1985 could be ordered with 3 proof-of-purchase coupons; however, this year $2.49 was the cost. The wheels and tires on 4 vehicles were altered as in 1985 to be accepted for "Under 3" usage. Not all stores received all 4 "Under 3" vehicles. Writing on the "Under 3" polybags was in red. Each Mini Stomper measured $1^3/_4$" x $2^3/_4$" x $1^1/_2$" and had rotating wheels. A track was designed on each of the 4 boxes which could be linked together to create a larger track.

Premiums

ST5575	Chevy S-10 Pick Up, black, Week 1	2 - 6
ST5576	Chevy S-10 Pick Up, yellow, Week 1	2 - 6
ST5577	Jeep Renegade, maroon, Week 1	2 - 6
ST5578	Jeep Renegade, orange, Week 1	2 - 6
ST5579	Chevy Van, red, Week 2	2 - 6
ST5580	Chevy Van, yellow, Week 2	2 - 6
ST5581	Dodge Rampage Pick Up, blue, Week 2	2 - 6
ST5582	Dodge Rampage Pick Up, white, Week 2	2 - 6
ST5583	Chevy Blazer 4x4, yellow, Week 3	2 - 6
ST5584	Chevy Blazer 4x4, red, Week 3	2 - 6
ST5585	AMC Eagle, black, Week 3	2 - 6
ST5586	AMC Eagle, orange, Week 3	2 - 6
ST5587	Ford Ranger Pick Up, orange, Week 4	2 - 6
ST5588	Ford Ranger Pick Up, red, Week 4	2 - 6
ST5589	Toyota Tercel 4x4, blue, Week 4	2 - 6
ST5590	Toyota Tercel 4x4, gray, Week 4	2 - 6
ST5591	Chevy Van, yellow (Under 3)	3 - 15
ST5592	Chevy Blazer, yellow (Under 3)	3 - 15
ST5593	Jeep Renegade, orange (Under 3)	3 - 15
ST5594	Toyota Tercel, blue (Under 3)	3 - 15

Boxes

ST5600	Jalopy Jump	2 - 4
ST5601	Quicksand Alley	2 - 4
ST5602	Rambunctious Ramp	2 - 4
ST5603	Thunderbolt Pass	2 - 4

Point of Purchase

ST5610	Translite, menu board, vacuformed for dimensional rugged look	10 - 15
ST5611	Translite, drive-thru	6 - 8
ST5612	Message Center Insert	8 - 10
ST5613	Counter Display w/premiums	75 - 100

STORY OF TEXAS, 1986

Shearer Publishing, Fredericksburg, TX, copyrighted the 4 *Story of Texas* history books used as premiums in a Texas

ST5600   ST5601   ST5602   ST5603

ST5611

ST5866

regional Happy Meal in 1986. There were 2 sets of the 50-page 5¹/₂" x 8¹/₂" books. Each book in each set contained the McDonald's logo on the front cover, inside front cover and back page. Also on the front cover of each book was the logo for a local TV station. One set featured KTVV-TV Austin, Channel 36; the other, KPRC-TV Houston, Channel 2. A 22" x 26" color "Discover the Story of Texas" map with the McDonald's logo in the right bottom corner came with each book in the Happy Meal. Shearer Publishing also printed the books without the McDonald's logo for their own distribution.

Premiums

ST5801	*The Story of Texas – Part 1: The Beginning*	3 - 10
ST5802	*The Story of Texas – Part 2: Independence*	3 - 10
ST5803	*The Story of Texas – Part 3: The Frontier*	3 - 10
ST5804	*The Story of Texas – Part 4: The 20th Century*	3 - 10
ST5805	Discover the Story of Texas map	3 - 6

Box

ST5808	Alamo/Armadillo	8 - 10

Point of Purchase

ST5815	Translite, menu board	15 - 20
ST5816	Translite, drive-thru	10 - 12

STORYBOOK MUPPET BABIES, 1988

Three soft cover Muppet Babies Storybooks, made exclusively for McDonald's, were the premiums for a national Happy Meal from Oct 28 to Nov 17, 1988. This Happy Meal promotion ran concurrently with McDonald's selling 3 Muppet Babies

plush dolls as a fund raiser for the Ronald McDonald House. The doll and book character matched each week. Each 24-page storybook measured 7" x 7" and contained 2 pages of tear-out coupons for Muppet Babies merchandise available from companies which produced these items. The American Library Association also took part in this promotion. A cut-out temporary library card was printed on each box and kids were encouraged to take this card to their local public library to exchange it for their own library card.

Premiums

ST5850	*Just Kermit and Me*, Baby Fozzie, Week 1	1 - 3
ST5851	*The Legend of Gimme Gulch*, Baby Kermit, Week 2	1 - 3
ST5852	*The Living Doll*, Baby Piggy, Week 3	1 - 3

ST5850   ST5851

ST5808

ST5804 (KPRC-TV)

ST5803 (KTVU-TV)

ST5852

ST5861	ST5860	ST5862

Boxes

ST5860	Library	1 - 3
ST5861	Nursery	1 - 3
ST5862	Picnic	1 - 3

Point of Purchase

ST5865	Translite, menu board	8 - 10
ST5866	Translite, drive-thru	6 - 8
ST5867	Menu Board Lug-On	6 - 8

SUMMER SURPRISE, 1990

During the summer of 1990, there were several weeks of clean-up where stores used leftover premiums supplied by McDonald's Corp. from their warehouses. The price was $1.99 for the Happy Meal; 2 generic sacks and a translite were used.

Sacks

SU5101	Ronald's Good Time Meal	1 - 3
SU5102	McDonald's Happy Meal, Ronald	1 - 3

Point of Purchase

SU5105	Translite, A Smile in Every Box, menu board	8 - 10
SU5106	Translite, A Smile in Every Box, drive-thru	6 - 8

SUPER GT (See MATCHBOX SUPER GT, 1988)

SU5105

SUPER LOONEY TUNES, 1991

Warner Bros. Super Looney Tunes characters were featured in a national Happy, Nov 8 to Dec 6, 1991. Each premium came in their original form, but with an add-on 2-part suit they became a super character. For the "Under 3" offering, the soft rubber figure was a 1-piece construction. The polybag also included a small comic book with a story about the character.

Premiums

SU7025	Bugs Bunny/Super Bugs, red/blue Batman suit	1 - 3
SU7026	Tasmanian Devil/Taz-Flash, red Devil suit	1 - 3
SU7027	Petunia Pig/Wonder Pig, red/white/blue Wonder Woman suit	1 - 3
SU7028	Daffy Duck/Bat-Duck, blue/gray Batman suit	1 - 3
SU7029	Daffy Duck/Bat-Duck in Batcar, blue (Under 3)	2 - 4

SU7025	SU7026	SU7027	SU7028	SU7029

Sack, 6" x 13"

SU7030	Maze	1 - 2

Point of Purchase

SU7035	Translite, menu board	8 - 10
SU7036	Translite, drive-thru	6 - 8
SU7037	Counter Display w/premiums	60 - 90

SU5101

SU7030

SU7110   SU7111   SU7112

SU7037

SUPER MARIO BROTHERS, 1990

This popular Nintendo video game was the theme for a national Happy Meal Aug 3–20, 1990. The McDonald premiums featured the main characters with action portraying their personality. Each came polybagged with an insert card.

Premiums

SU7101	Mario, he pops up when pressed down, Set 1	1 - 3
SU7102	Luigi, pull him back and he races forward doing twists & turns, Set 2	1 - 3
SU7103	Little Goomba, press him down & he does a back flip, Set 3	1 - 3
SU7104	Koopa Paratroop, press the bellows & he bumps around, Set 4	1 - 3
SU7105	Mario, squeeze toy (Under 3)	2 - 4

Boxes

SU7110	Desert Land	1 - 3
SU7111	Island World	1 - 3
SU7112	Pipe Land	1 - 3
SU7113	Sky Land	1 - 3

Point of Purchase

SU7118	Translite, menu board	8 - 10
SU7119	Translite, drive-thru	6 - 8
SU7120	Counter Display w/premiums	60 - 90
SU7121	Danglers, 1 for each premium, each	4 - 6
SU7122	Tray Liner	1 - 3

SU7101   SU7102   SU7103   SU7104   SU7105

SU7113   SU5710   SU7120

SU7118

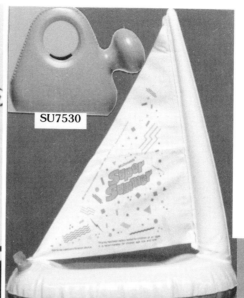

SU7530

SU7544

SU7501

SUPER SUMMER, 1987, Test

The test for the Super Summer Happy Meal was conducted in Fresno, CA from May 22 through June 25, 1987. Though the test ran for 5 weeks, details on only 1 premium are known.

SU7529

SU7527

Premium

SU7501	Inflatable Sailboat	10 - 20
Sack, 8" x 12"		
SU7510	Super Summer	8 - 10

SU7525

SU7528

SU7526

SU7535

SU7542

SUPER SUMMER, 1988

Toys to be used outside during the summer time were the premiums in a national Super Summer Happy Meal, May 26 to June 23, 1988. Two plastic inflatable toys came in polybags and 3 hard plastic toys made up the 5 premiums. A 1-piece blue watering can was originally scheduled and was included in the first samples and translite sent to the stores. At the last minute, this was replaced by a blue fish mold. Stores received a sample of the fish mold and new translites showing the mold instead of the watering can. One sack was used for all the premiums except the sand pails. The sailboat differed from the test case offering in that Grimace was placed on the sail, the strap holding the back of the sail to the boat was thicker and less red was used in the graphics.

155

TA6510 TA6511 TA6512 TA6513

SU7540

Premiums

SU7525	Sand Pail w/Rake, white w/yellow rake, handle, sand sifter lid, Week 1	1 - 3
SU7526	Beach Ball, inflatable, white, 14½", Week 2	2 - 4
SU7527	Sailboat, inflatable, Grimace, Week 3	2 - 4
SU7528	Fish Sand Mold, blue, Week 4	1 - 3
SU7529	Sand Castle Pail w/Shovel, white w/red shovel, handle, sand sifter lid, Week 5	1 - 3
SU7530	Watering Can, blue (cancelled premium)	20 - 30

Sack, 8½" x 12"

SU7535	Picnic Puzzler	1 - 3

Point of Purchase

SU7540	Translite, menu board w/fish mold	8 - 10
SU7541	Translite, drive-thru w/fish mold	6 - 8
SU7542	Translite, menu board w/watering can	10 - 15
SU7543	Translite, drive-thru w/watering can	8 - 12
SU7544	Floor Display w/premiums	60 - 80

SUPER TRAVELERS (See LEGO BUILDING SETS (Little Travelers), 1985)

TALE SPIN, 1990

In the fall of 1990, "Tale Spin" joined the Disney afternoon TV line-up. In the animated series Baloo the Bear and his friends become pilots and exciting adventure takes place as villains try to stop them from delivering their cargo. This was the first national Happy Meal to use die cast premiums. Four airplanes with turning characters, propellers and wheels and 2 soft PVC "Under 3" airplanes were the premiums for this Nov 2 to Nov 29, 1990 promotion. Each came in a printed polybag.

Premiums

TA6501	Baloo's Seaplane, orange/gold, Week 1	1 - 3
TA6502	Molly's Biplane, red, Week 2	1 - 3
TA6503	Kit's Racing Plane, blue/orange, Week 3	1 - 3
TA6504	Wildcat's Flying Machine, green, Week 4	1 - 3
TA6505	Baloo's Seaplane, orange (Under 3)	2 - 4
TA6506	Wildcat's Flying Machine, green (Under 3)	2 - 4

TA6501   TA6503   TA6502   TA6504   TA6505   TA6506

Boxes

TA6510	Higher For Hire	1 - 3
TA6511	Louies	1 - 3
TA6512	Pirate Island	1 - 3
TA6513	Sea Duck	1 - 3

Point of Purchase

TA6520	Translite, menu board	8 - 10
TA6521	Translite, drive-thru	6 - 8
TA6522	Counter Display w/premiums, motion	75 - 100
TA6523	Ceiling Dangler, 1 for each character	4 - 6

TA6522

TALKING STORYBOOK (See DINOSAURS (Talking Storybook, 1989)

156

TH5556   TH5557   TI5515

TH5558   TH5555   TI5523   TI5523

TA6520

TH5550

TH5565

3–D HAPPY MEAL, 1981

This regional promotion ran in either May–June or Nov. 2–29, 1981. It is known to have run in all or part of AR, KS, MS, MO, OK, and TN. The 3-D cardboard glasses had cellophane lens with the right eye piece being blue and the left one red. Frames were shaped like the Golden Arches with small *M*'s on the ear piece. On a local option basis, stores could give out an additional generic premium to offset potential disappointment among repeat purchasers. Four boxes featured 3-D artwork based on photos, courtesy of the University of Missouri at Kansas City Special Collections Department.

Premiums

TH5550	3-D Glasses only	8 - 10

Boxes

TH5555	Bugsville/Hungry Funnies	15 - 25
TH5556	High Jinx/Clownish Capers	15 - 25
TH5557	Locomotion/Laughing Stock	15 - 25

TI5520

TH5558	Space Follies/Gurgle Gags	15 - 25
TH5559	TH5555-58 w/glasses	25 - 35
Point of Purchase		
TH5565	Translite, menu board/drive-thru (large)	20 - 30

TINOSAURS, 1986

Characters from the wondrous Isle of Tiny (which was featured on a Saturday morning TV show) provided the premiums for the Tinosaurs Happy Meal. This ran on a regional basis in parts of MO, NE, AR, TN, AL and MS from Sept 12 to Oct 19, 1986. The 8 hard rubber characters were painted and each one had a yellow *M* in a prominent place. All were issued in a polybag printed with safety information. Tinosaurs are copyrighted by Aviva Enterprises and licensed by Prime Designs Licensing, Ltd.

Premiums

TI5501	Bones, the merriest Tinosaur, green	3 - 8
TI5502	Dinah, the wisest Tinosaur, orange	3 - 8
TI5503	Fern, the loveable time traveler, white	3 - 8
TI5504	Jad, the baby dragon, purple	3 - 8
TI5505	Kobby, the Kave Kolt, purple w/green hair & white feet	3 - 8
TI5506	Link, an acrobatic elf, purple	3 - 8
TI5507	Spell, the nasty Gumpies leader, blue w/green hands	3 - 8
TI5508	Tiny, a not-so-tiny Tinosaur, purple	3 - 8

TI5501 TI5502 TI5503 TI5504 TI5505 TI5506 TI5507 TI5508

Box
TI5515	Tinosaurs	3 - 6
Point of Purchase		
TI5520	Translite, menu board	10 - 15
TI5521	Translite, drive-thru	10 - 12
TI5522	Counter Mat	6 - 8
TI5523	Table Tent	3 - 5

TI5822

TINY TOON, 1991

Warner Brothers and McDonald's began a new tie-in with this Feb 8 – Mar 7, 1991 Happy Meal. It featured all 8 leading characters from the Steven Spielberg–produced Saturday morning animated TV series, "Tiny Toon Adventures". The show characters came from Wackyland and attended ACME Looniversity. The promotion used a new kind of premium called "Flip Cars". In essence, these were 2 toys in one as when the car was flipped over a different type of character and car appeared. Two wheels of each vehicle matched the theme of one side of the flip car, the other two wheels matched the other.

Premiums
| TI5801 | Babs Bunny in Phone/Plucky Duck in Boat, Week 1 | 1 - 3 |

TI5821

TI5820

TI5810   TI5811

TI5812   TI5813

TI5801   TI5802   TI5803   TI5804

TI5805   TI5806

TI5500   TI5504

TI5501   TI5502   TI5503

TI5802	Elmira Pig in Wagon/Buster Bunny in Carrot, Week 2	1 - 3
TI5803	Montana Max in Car/Gogo Dodo in Bathtub, Week 3	1 - 3
TI5804	Hampton Pig in Hero Sandwich/Dizzy Devil in Amplifier, Week 4	1 - 3
TI5805	Gogo Dodo in Bathtub, soft PVC (Under 3)	2 - 4
TI5806	Plucky Duck in Boat, soft PVC (Under 3)	2 - 4
Boxes		
TI5810	Acme Acres	1 - 3
TI5811	Forest	1 - 3
TI5812	Looniversity	1 - 3
TI5813	Wackyland	1 - 3
Point of Purchase		
TI5820	Translite, menu board, thick plastic, X-O graphic	10 - 20
TI5821	Translite, drive-thru	6 - 8
TI5822	Counter Display w/premiums	60 - 90

TOM & JERRY BAND, 1990

Tom & Jerry cartoon characters playing instruments in a band were the premiums for a regional Happy Meal. The promotion first ran in Southern CA in Jan 1990; later in Northern CA from Sept 7 to Oct 4, 1990. For the "Under 3" premium the Spike figure alone was used placed in the "Under 3" polybag. Two different sizes of bags were tested. Each had the same graphics in black, red and white, but the smaller one added yellow.

Premiums		
TO5500	Tom w/keyboard, 4 pcs, Set 1	4 - 8
TO5501	Droopy w/microphone, 2 pcs – mike moves up and down, Set 2	4 - 8
TO5502	Jerry w/drum set, 2 pcs, stool spins, Set 3	4 - 8
TO5503	Spike w/bass, 2 pcs, Set 4	4 - 8
TO5504	Droopy, 1 pc w/o mike (Under 3)	- - 10
Sacks		
TO5508	Larger sack	3 - 5
TO5509	Smaller sack	1 - 3
Point of Purchase		
TO5515	Translite, menu board	10 - 15
TO5516	Translite, drive-thru	8 - 12

TO5601

TOOTHBRUSH, 1985

Ronald McDonald toothbrushes in 3 different colors were given out as Happy Meal premiums in a regional promotion. The toothbrush has a 1984 copyright date, while the translite carries a 1985 copyright. A full figure Ronald is on the end of

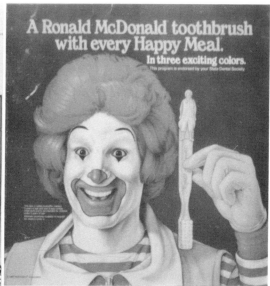

TO5608

TO5515

TO5509

the handle and the name "Ronald McDonald" is on the side of the handle. Each toothbrush came in a polybag with "Ronald McDonald tootbrush. Safety tested for children 3 years and older" and the McDonald's logo printed on it. The translite reads, "This program is endorsed by your State Dental Society."

Premiums

TO5601	Ronald toothbrush, yellow	3 - 10
TO5602	Ronald toothbrush, red	3 - 10
TO5603	Ronald toothbrush, ?	3 - 10

Point of Purchase

TO5608	Translite, menu board	15 - 25

TRANSFORMERS/MY LITTLE PONY, 1985

A St. Louis regional Happy Meal featured toys by Hasbro Badley, Inc in May 1985. This unusual promotion had separate premiums for boys and girls. Counting all the color variations, there were a total of 30 premiums.

The boy's premium was a 1-piece transformer with no moveable parts. Each of the 4 different transformers came in 6 different color combinations. Inside each polybag was a flier with a mail-back coupon. For 3 proof-of-purchase coupons and $5.99 plus $1 shipping charges, an Overdrive Transformer could be purchased.

Six My Little Pony clip-on charms were the girl's premium. Inside the polybag was a flier with a proof-of-purchase coupon. With 3 coupons, $3.99 plus $1 shipping, a Birthflower Pony could be ordered – choice of 12 different ones available.

The box was designed with transformer graphics on one side; My Little Pony graphics on the other.

Premiums – Transformer Figures

TR0601	Brawn – blue/yellow, green/blue, green/ yellow, red/blue, red/green, red/yellow	8 - 15

TR0602	Bumblebee – black/blue, black/green, black/red, violet/blue, wine/black, yellow/ black	8 - 15
TR0603	Cliffjumper – black/blue, black/green, black/red, violet/blue, wine/black, yellow/ black	8 - 15
TR0604	Gears – blue/yellow, green/blue, green/ yellow, red/blue, red/green, red/yellow	8 - 15

TR6010   TR6011   TR6012   TR6013   TR6014   TR6015

TR6025

TRO601   TRO602   TRO603   TRO604

TR6020   TRO6020 (other side)   TR6026 (Transformers side)

Premiums – My Little Pony

TR6010	Blossom, purple pony w/flower imprint	6 - 15
TR6011	Blue Belle, blue gray pony w/star imprint	6 - 15
TR6012	Butterscotch, butterscotch pony w/butterfly imprint	6 - 15
TR6013	Cotton Candy, pink pony w/paw print imprint	6 - 15
TR6014	Minty, green pony w/3 leaf clover imprint	6 - 15
TR6015	Snuzzle, gray w/heart imprint	6 - 15

Box

TR6020	Transformer Figure/My Little Pony Charm	4 - 6

Point of Purchase

TR6025	Translite	10 - 15
TR6026	Table Tent	4 - 6
TR6027	Tray Liner	4 - 6

TURBO MACS, 1988

Turbo-Macs ran as a regional Happy Meal in 1988 and again in 1989. Each of the 4 pull-back vehicles carried a McDonaldland character. All premiums were polybagged with an insert card. The "Under 3" polybag did not contain an insert card.

Premiums

TU7120	Birdie, pink sports car, brown hair, small yellow M on front of car	3 - 6
TU7121	Grimace, white Indy type car, large yellow	3 - 6

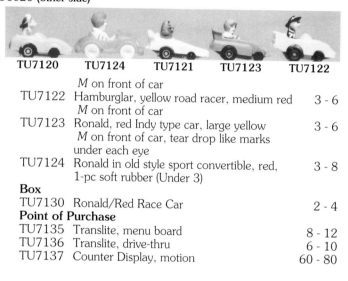

TU7120   TU7124   TU7121   TU7123   TU7122

	M on front of car	
TU7122	Hamburglar, yellow road racer, medium red M on front of car	3 - 6
TU7123	Ronald, red Indy type car, large yellow M on front of car, tear drop like marks under each eye	3 - 6
TU7124	Ronald in old style sport convertible, red, 1-pc soft rubber (Under 3)	3 - 8

Box

TU7130	Ronald/Red Race Car	2 - 4

Point of Purchase

TU7135	Translite, menu board	8 - 12
TU7136	Translite, drive-thru	6 - 10
TU7137	Counter Display, motion	60 - 80

TURBO MACS, 1990

Once again Turbo Macs ran as a regional promotion in 1990, but this time each of the 4 regular vehicles had slight changes. All premiums came with an insert card in the polybag. The box and the translites are the same as those used in 1988 (see TU7130, TU7135 and TU7136).

TU7137

TU7123   TU7203

TU7130

TR6026 (My Little Pony side)

UN3135

UN3136

UNDERSEA, 1980

Exploring the depths of the sea was the theme for the Undersea Happy Meal in the spring of 1980. For this national option campaign, McDonald's Corporation developed 6 boxes. Each market was allowed to determine their own premiums. The St. Louis market used Diener soft rubber sea animal figures which are listed below. These figures were also sold in retail stores. Other areas' offerings are unknown. The name "Undersea" is not on the front of the boxes, but it is on the translite and counter card.

Premiums

UN3101	Alligator	50¢ - 1
UN3102	Dolphin	50¢ - 1
UN3103	Seal	50¢ - 1
UN3104	Shark, Great White	50¢ - 1
UN3105	Shark, Hammerhead	50¢ - 1
UN3106	Shark, Tiger	50¢ - 1
UN3107	Shark, Whale	50¢ - 1
UN3108	Turtle	50¢ - 1
UN3109	Walrus	50¢ - 1
UN3110	Whale	50¢ - 1

Boxes

UN3135	Captain/Ronald	10 - 15
UN3136	Grimace/Diver	10 - 15
UN3137	Grimace/Porpoise	10 - 15

UN3101   UN3102   UN3103   UN3104   UN3105

UN3106   UN3107   UN3108   UN3109   UN3110

TU7135

Premiums

TU7200	Birdie, pink sports car, red hair, large yellow *M* on front of car	2 - 4
TU7201	Grimace, white Indy type car, large red *M* on front of car	2 - 4
TU7202	Hamburglar, yellow road racer, large red *M* on front of car	2 - 4
TU7203	Ronald, red Indy type car, large yellow *M* on front of car	2 - 4
TU7204	Same as TU7124 except packaging	3 - 5

TV LUNCH BUNCH (See LUNCH BOX (TV Lunch Bunch), 1987)

UN3137   UN3138   UN3139

WA0520

teen/adult business.

UN3145

UN3138	Secret Message/Seashell	10 - 15
UN3139	Ronald/Submarine	10 - 15
UN3140	(topic unknown)	10 - 15
Point of Purchase		
UN3145	Translite, menu board/drive-thru (large)	20 - 25
UN3146	Counter Card (see back cover)	15 - 20
UN3147	Ceiling Dangler	50 - 75

UNIDENTIFIED HAPPY MEAL (See SPACESHIP (Unidentified Happy Meal), 1981, Test)

UNITED (See FRIENDLY SKIES, 1991)

VALENTINE (See FROM THE HEART, 1990)

WACKY, 1982

"Wacky" activities were featured on the boxes used in a regional promotion in the St. Louis area from Mar 1 to May 23, 1982. The 6 boxes themselves were the premiums as they offered a variety of funny and silly entertainment such as: Wacky Maze, Wacky Band, Wacky Bowling, Wacky Writing, Wacky Watch, Wacky Wheel, Wacky Dancers and Wacky Bird Call, plus many others. Though called "Wacky", the activites were also educational. Six 8-oz white plastic cups were used as a possible premium or used as a self-liquidator to attract more

Premiums/Boxes

WA0501	Farm	10 - 15
WA0502	Forest	10 - 15
WA0503	Party	10 - 15
WA0504	Parade	10 - 15
WA0505	Picnic	10 - 15
WA0506	Zoo	10 - 15
Cups		
WA0510	Airplane Hanger	2 - 5
WA0511	Country Club	2 - 5
WA0512	Figure Skating	2 - 5
WA0513	Jungle Gym	2 - 5
WA0514	Monkey Business	2 - 5
WA0515	Traffic Jam	2 - 5
Point of Purchase		
WA0520	Translite, menu board/drive-thru (large)	15 - 20
WA0521	Permanent Display Header Card	8 - 10

WATER GAMES, 1992

Hand-held Water Games were one of the offerings in the 1992 Open Window, Feb 7 to Mar 6. After filling the water compartment, pressure applied to the button on the front created "currents" which would cause the small pieces inside to float around. Object of the game was to catch the small pieces in holding slots. Each polybag was printed with the promotion information and the background stripes on the package

WA0501   WA0502   WA0503

WA0504 WA0505 WA0506

WA0510 WA0511 WA0512 WA0513 WA0514 WA0515

matched the color of the game. Problems arose and during the first week a flyer was printed and distributed with further instructions for proper use. The "Under 3" premium, a soft rubber Grimace with Squirting Camera, was recalled (reason unknown) the first day of the promotion. Some areas did not give away premiums #3 or #4.

Premiums

WA8001	Ronald Catching French Fries, yellow, #1	1 - 3
WA8002	Grimace Juggling Shakes, green, #2	1 - 3
WA8003	Hamburglar Stacking Burgers, orange, #3	2 - 4
WA8004	Birdie Sorting Eggs, hot pink, #4	2 - 4
WA8005	Grimace w/Squirting Camera, 1-pc, purple	2 - 5

Sack, 6" x 12"

WA8010	Ronald/Dot-to-Dot!	1 - 3

Point of Purchase

WA8015	Translite, menu board	10 - 12
WA8016	Translite, drive-thru	8 - 10

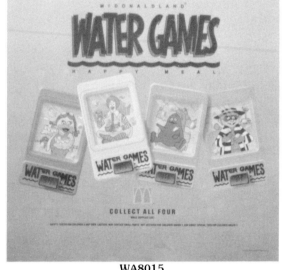

WA8015

WA8001 WA8002 WA8004 WA8003 WA8005

WILD FRIENDS, 1992

In the Indianapolis and LA regions, the Open Window (Feb 7 – Mar 6, 1992) premiums featured animals placed on the Endangered Species list. Each animal was firmly attached to a plastic base which formed the back cover and spine of the miniature comic book glued to the underneath side of the base. The comic book provided information and fun facts about the animal and its environment. There was a moveable piece on each animal: the head turned on the panda and elephant; the mouth opened slightly on the crocodile; the gorilla's arm moved. The "Under 3" premium was a 1-piece, soft rubber Giant Panda. No comic book came with this offering. Polybags were used and came with an insert card entitled "Wild Animal Toy Books". The term "Wild Friends" appeared on the sack and the translites.

Premiums

WI4501	Elephant, gray/green base, #1	1 - 3

WA8010

WI4510

WI4502	Crocodile, green/pink base, #2	1 - 3
WI4503	Gorilla, gray/yellow base, #3	1 - 3
WI4504	Giant Panda, black & white/blue base, #4	1 - 3
WI4505	Giant Panda (Under 3)	1 - 4

Sack, 6" x 12"

WI4510	4 Wild Friends	1 - 3

Point of Purchase

WI4515	Translite, menu board	10 - 12
WI4516	Translite, drive-thru	8 - 10

WI4515

WI6110   WI6111

WI6101   WI6102   WI6103   WI6104   WI6105

WI4501   WI4502   WI4503   WI4504   WI4505

WINTER WORLDS, 1983/84

The Winter Worlds Happy Meal, a national option from Nov 28, 1983 to Feb 5, 1984, suggested the use of five 4" vinyl McDonaldland figures for the premiums. A string loop on each full color character would enable it to be used as an ornament on a Christmas tree or as a decoration year round. The figures carried a 1983 copyright. However, some areas developed their own premiums. The 5 boxes were designed with graphics of the winter theme. In 1984, these same premiums were issued bearing a 1984 copyright and were used as give-aways.

Premiums

WI6101	Birdie, 1983 copyright	3 - 6
WI6102	Grimace, 1983 copyright	3 - 6
WI6103	Hamburglar, 1983 copyright	3 - 6
WI6104	Major McCheese, 1983 copyright	3 - 6
WI6105	Ronald, 1983 copyright	3 - 6

Boxes

WI6110	Birds of Ice and Snow	5 - 7
WI6111	Lands of Ice and Snow	5 - 7
WI6112	Lands of the Midnight Sun	5 - 7
WI6113	Mammals of the Icy Shores	5 - 7
WI6114	People of the Frosty Frontier	5 - 7

Point of Purchase

WI6118	Translite, menu board/drive-thru (large)	10 - 15
WI6119	Message Center Insert, cardboard	10 - 15
WI6120	Permanent Display Header Card	4 - 6
WI6121	Menu Board Premium Lug-On	4 - 6

YO, YOGI!, 1992

Yogi Bear and friends were featured for the first time in a McDonald's Happy Meal during the Open Window, Feb 7 – Mar 6, 1992, in the northern CA area. The premiums consisted of 1-piece rev-up action toys – a figure in a vehicle – and came polybagged with a 1-color insert card. All were recommended for children age 1 and over. The insert card and figures each have a 1991 Hanna-Barbera Productions, Inc. copyright; however, the sack bears the 1992 Turner Broadcasting System, Inc./Turner Home Entertainment, Inc. copyright.

Premiums

YO4501	Yogi/LAF Squad Wave Jumper, orange	1 - 5
YO4502	Huckleberry Hound/LAF Squad Race Car, yellow	1 - 5
YO4503	Cindy Bear/LAF Squad Scooter, green	1 - 5
YO4504	Boo Boo Bear/LAF Squad Skate Board, blue	1 - 5

Sack, 6" x 12"

YO4510	Yogi/Jellystone Park	1 - 3

WI6112   WI6113   WI6114

WI6118

Point of Purchase
YO4515 Translite, menu board   10 - 12
YO4516 Translite, drive-thru   8 - 10

YOUNG ASTRONAUTS, 1986

Following a suggestion by prize–winning columnist Jack Anderson to set up a program to encourage students and teachers to excel in math, science and technology, President Ronald Reagan established the Young Astronauts Program on June 19, 1984. McDonald's began a 2-year commitment to this program in 1986. From Sept 8 to Oct 5, four plastic space

YO4501   YO4502   YO4503   YO4504

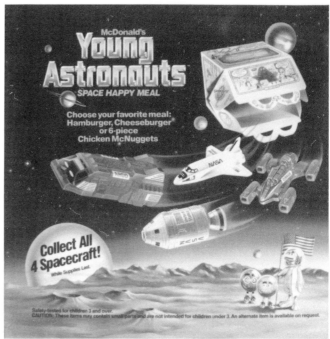

YO7118

vehicles, made exclusively for McDonald's by Monogram Models, an official licensee of the Young Astronauts Council, were used as the regular premiums. Each one measured 3" - 4" and included a decal sheet in the polybag. Two 1-piece air-planes were recommended for children under 3. On the Moonbase box the "Lunar Lookout" lettering was printed in blue and also in pink.

Premiums
YO7101 Apollo Command Module, gray, 2 pcs   5 - 8
YO7102 Argo Land Shuttle, red, 1 pc   5 - 8
YO7103 Cirrus VTOL (Vertical Take-Off and Landing), 5 - 8
        blue, 1 pc
YO7104 Space Shuttle, white, 1 pc   5 - 8
        Fry Guy Friendly Flyer (see AI6066)
        Grimace Smiling Shuttle (see AI6067)

YO7101   YO7102   YO7103   YO7104

YO4515   YO4510

YO7110

YO7111　　　　　　　　YO7112　　　　　　　　YO7113

Boxes

YO7110	Mars Adventure	2 - 5
YO7111	Moonbase	2 - 5
YO7112	Repair Station	2 - 5
YO7113	Space Station	2 - 5

Point of Purchase

YO7118	Translite, menu board/drive-thru (large)	10 - 12
YO7119	Translite, drive-thru (small)	8 - 10
YO7120	Message Center Insert, cardboard	10 - 12

ZOO–FACE, 1987, Test

Zoo-Face animal nose masks were tested in the Evansville, IN area from Oct 2 – 31, 1987. Each rubber mask came bagged with a Paas make-up kit bearing a 1987 date. The "Under 3" paper die-cut X-O graph mask also came bagged with a make-up kit. The boxes and point of purchase displays which were used in this promotion have not been identified.

Premiums

ZO5501	Alligator	10 - 20
ZO5502	Monkey	10 - 20
ZO5503	Tiger	10 - 20
ZO5504	Toucan	10 - 20
ZO5505	Tiger, paper mask, dated 1987 (Under 3)	10 - 20

ZO5505

Boxes

ZO5610	Ape House	1 - 3
ZO5611	Bird House	1 - 3
ZO5612	Lion House	1 - 3
ZO5613	Reptile House	1 - 3

Point of Purchase

ZO5620	Translite, menu board	8 - 10
ZO5621	Translite, drive-thru	6 - 8

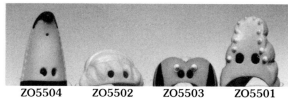

ZO5504　　ZO5502　　ZO5503　　ZO5501

ZOO–FACE, 1988

The national Zoo-Face Happy Meal was offered from Sept 30 to Oct 27, 1988. Several changes were incorporated after the 1987 test. The thin elastic string was replaced by a heavier elastic string. Air holes in all 4 masks were enlarged; the alligator and toucan masks were reshaped and the number of holes changed from 2 to 3. Each Paas 3-color face paint for the regular premiums was numbered. All regular premiums were polybagged with an insert card. Two 1988 copyrighted X-O graph paper masks, issued in a clear polybag without face paint or insert card, were used for "Under 3" premiums.

Premiums

ZO5601	Toucan, Week 1	1 - 3
ZO5602	Monkey, Week 2	1 - 3
ZO5603	Tiger, Week 3	1 - 3
ZO5604	Alligator, Week 4	1 - 3
ZO5605	Monkey, dated 1988 (Under 3)	3 - 6
ZO5606	Tiger, dated 1988 (Under 3)	3 - 6

ZO5620

ZO5610   ZO5611   ZO5612

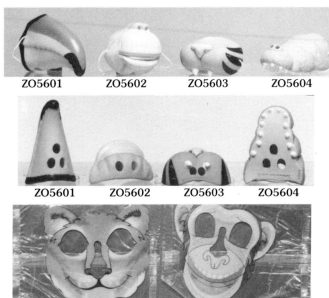

ZO5601   ZO5602   ZO5603   ZO5604

ZO5601   ZO5602   ZO5603   ZO5604

ZO5606   ZO5605

ZO5613

Meredith Williams

ABOUT THE AUTHOR

Meredith Williams began collecting McDonald's memorabilia in 1980 and was fortunate to live close to one of the original test markets for the Happy Meal concept. He traveled extensively with a local college music group and noticed the different Happy Meals offerings in various parts of the country. A chance comment by his brother on collecting McDonald's items and the vast amount of material available captured his interest and he was hooked.

Early on he began writing down this information to record accurate dates and other data for his own collecting interest. Meredith began to share his findings with other collectors in January 1989, by publishing the first issue of the *Collecting Tips Newsletter* for McDonald's collectors. This helped him establish a network with other collectors and obtain McDonald's memorabilia not available in his travels.

His growing interest coincided with McDonald's establishing a permanent archives for the corporation. Over the years he has visited the archives many times to verify findings and share discoveries.

The results of Meredith's collecting and research are now published in *Tomart's Price Guide to McDonald's HAPPY MEAL Collectibles*, his first book.

Meredith is married and lives in Joplin, Missouri. He and his wife, Heather, have three sons – Mark, Brian and Nathan.